THE
KNOT BOOK

by

GEOFFREY BUDWORTH

PAPERFRONTS
ELLIOT RIGHT WAY BOOKS,
KINGSWOOD, SURREY, U.K.

Made and Printed in Great Britain by
Richard Clay Ltd., Bungay, Suffolk.

HOW TO USE THIS BOOK

The list of contents at the beginning, in chapter and page order, will show you where to look for a history of ropemaking, techniques and terms, basic knots, string knots, more general knots, anglers' knots, climbers' knots, various other knots, new knots and trick knots.

A list of illustrations follows. If you know the name of a knot or a technique and want to see what it looks like, run your eye quickly down this list to spot the page you need.

If you know roughly what you want to achieve — but don't know the right knot for the job — look at the 'Knots, according to use' section also at the front — where you will find listed the names of knots for joining the ends of lines together; knots for attaching a line to a rail, post, another line, etc.; knots tied in the ends of lines as stopper knots; binding knots; single loop knots tied in the end of lines; loop knots tied in the bight of lines without using ends; multiple loop knots tied in the end of lines for rescues, salvage, etc; and knots for various other purposes.

Knotting terms, where necessary, are fully explained in the text and also appear in a glossary at the end of the book.

To James Nicoll from Largo in the Kingdom of Fife, still the best knotsman I've ever met, for his friendship and knowledge.

In the same series:

Upholstery Properly Explained
Dressmaking In Pictures
Fly Dressing and Some Tackle Making
Make Your Own Fishing Tackle
Begin Cruising Under Sail

Each uniform with this book.

CONTENTS

ILLUSTRATIONS

KNOTS — according to use

KNOTS FOR JOINING THE ENDS OF LINES TOGETHER

KNOTS FOR ATTACHING A LINE TO A RAIL, POST, ANOTHER LINE, etc.

KNOTS TIED IN THE END OF LINES AS STOPPER KNOTS

BINDING KNOTS

SINGLE LOOP KNOTS IN THE END OF LINES

n.b. Starred (*) knots are sliding loops which may be adjusted to size

LOOP KNOTS TIED IN THE BIGHT OF LINES

MULTIPLE LOOP KNOTS TIED IN THE END OF LINES FOR RESCUES, SALVAGE, ETC.

KNOTS FOR VARIOUS OTHER PURPOSES

ACKNOWLEDGEMENTS

No one can be wholly original on knots. Too many others have drawn and written about them. I gratefully acknowledge all those sources from which I have — consciously or unconsciously — acquired my knotting know how.

My thanks go to Mr. J. C. Bates of British Ropes Ltd. for bringing together publisher and author; and to Mr. Peter Manners, the works manager, for his time and encouragement.

A number of friends within the International Guild of Knot Tyers have kindly given me permission to use their original ideas which I am pleased to portray and describe in print for the first time. I am especially indebted to Canadian climber and guide Bob Chisnall. My knowledge of climbers' knots was largely learned from him. He is also a clever knotting innovator. The Double Hedden Knot is his variation of an established knot. Hunter's Loop, the Adjustable Knot, and the Three Quarter Figure of Eight Loops are further examples of his inventiveness. The Double Munter Friction Hitch (which may also be called a Double Crossing Knot) is recommended as a climbers' knot but so far only infrequently adopted by them. His Ontario and Algonquin Bowlines are experiments — not in general climbing use — and (it should be noted) may be regarded as new knots.

It's hard to choose from the many knots by Desmond Mandeville, but I unhesitatingly introduce his Tumbling Thief Knot to the knotting scene, together with the Poor Man's Pride and also Bend 'X'. Ettrick W. Thomson has contributed his method of tying the Poor Man's Pride.

Others to whom I am indebted for their own original material are my younger daughter Julie for Julie's Hitch; Mr. John Sweet, lifelong scout, knotting writer and authority on pioneering with ropes and spars, for his modification of the Waggoner's Hitch with a strop; and Amory B. Lovins who — while working in Britain with Friends of the Earth Ltd. pointed out to me the real origin of Hunter's Bend — for his Vibration Proof Hitch.

I gratefully acknowledge the generosity of Mr. Spike Milligan for permission to reproduce his apt poem 'String' at the beginning of Chapter 5. This poem originally appeared in 'Silly Verse for Kids' by Spike Milligan, published by Penguin Books Ltd. (1959).

My sincere thanks also go to Malcolm Elliot for his patience and editorial guidance; and to James Lester, illustrator, for his skill and tenacity in coping with my original drawings.

INTRODUCTION

"It is extraordinary how little the average individual knows about the art of making even the simplest knots." (R. M. Abraham — 1932)

Imagine you are trapped on an upper floor of a burning building, too high to jump without serious injury. How can you improvise a rope? Tie bedsheets together and climb down them? It's been done . . . but what knot should you use?

Have you ever taken trouble tying an awkward load onto the luggage rack of your car, only to have it shift dangerously after just a few miles? Do you continually stop to re-tie your shoe laces? Is it difficult to re-string your children's musical instruments, or to make a parcel? Then you need to know the right knots.

We all have to fasten string or bandages sooner or later; and it's knots that make them work. Housewives or D.I.Y. hobbyists, gardeners or modelmakers, there are the right knots for us all. Whether you are a parent trying to amuse a toddlers' tea party, or a self-sufficiency exponent anxious to use the natural environment without depleting it, knots will help. You can learn to tie them at any age. One of the knots in this book was invented by a girl of 9 years; others by a grandfather. Acquiring skill with knots can be good therapy for the sick and the mentally or physically handicapped, or simply an absorbing pastime.

Many people cope for a long time without knowing any really useful knots but only because they can replace them with handy manufactured fastenings like safety pins, dog lead clasps, snap-links, screws, glue, and those elastic cords with metal hooks on the ends. Now they're fine when they're available — I use them all the time — but without them you're lost, unless you can tie a knot or two. Knots are a useful alternative in many circumstances and indispensable in others. That's why so many practical folk scorn spending money unnecessarily on gadgets and take pride in knowing the right knot for the job.

You don't have to like boats to enjoy knotting. Knot books tend to have a nautical flavour but that is only because old-time sailormen did more than any other group to develop practical knotting. Thus many knots and knotting terms are to do with ships and sailors. Don't be put off by that. The knots are just as useful ashore as they were afloat.

There are thousands of knots and an infinite number of variations of some of them. This book shows you about 100. The first half dozen or so are invaluable, used around the world by everyone who has to make rope, cord or string work for them. The wider selection that follows — and the specialised needs of rock climbers and anglers have even been catered for — are all very useful on occasions. Knots are like tools. You can't have too many; then you can always pick just the right one for the job.

(Incidentally, to tie those bedsheets together and so escape the fire, learn the Double Sheet Bend (fig. 14 (C)–(D) or the Fisherman's Knot (fig. 15) or the Surgeon's Knot (fig. 30).)

1

HISTORY

Cavemen tied knots. So did the Incas of Peru who made knotted strings instead of written figures to keep elaborate accounts. They may be man's oldest tool. Primitive peoples from Eskimos to South Pacific Indians needed knots; and the Ancient Persians, Greeks, Romans and Egyptians probably knew as much as us about them.

Knots were important to the Venetians who maintained their empire by maritime strength, and in the Middle Ages knotting also acquired religious symbolism and superstitions. Charlatans were punished for 'knot sorcery'. Renaissance genius Leonardo da Vinci designed a knotted fringe on the gown of the Mona Lisa. By the 18th century, when every clipper ship was a spider's web of rope rigging, illiterate seamen were producing masterpieces of knotted and braided ropework both practical and decorative. When commercial sailing ships died knotting seemed to die too.

Yet some people today still need knots. Rock climbers and potholers secure their nylon ropes with care. Their lives hang on them. Anglers — like climbers — are concerned with knot strengths but tie them in thin monofilaments. Amateur boatmen preserve the knots of the old sailormen but tie them in modern braided ropes. Sea fishermen continue to make and mend nets.

Archers may still make their own bowstrings. Bellringers, book binders, shoemakers and falconers all learn a knot or two peculiar to their callings. Firemen, riggers (in circus and theatre), steeplejacks and stevedores use knots as tools of their trades. Truck drivers use the Waggoner's Hitch (fig. 21 (B)), a tensioning device related to the Sheepshank (fig. 21 (F)), and we all need to tie shoe laces. Weavers, river workers and sail-makers keep the old knowledge alive, as do scouts and guides, sea cadets and rangers.

Some individuals find tying complicated knots as absorbing as completing any other sort of puzzle. Advanced mathematics students can study 'Knot Theory', a sort of

3-dimensional geometry; while designers use knot patterns to sell items as varied as book jackets, tea towels, dress fabrics and swim suits.

2
ROPEMAKING

In August, 1945, contractors blasting for building stone in the underground limestone quarries of Turah, near Cairo, discovered the mummified remains of workmen maybe employed in the construction of the Great Pyramids of Gizeh and Memphis. With them was a large 3-strand rope, presumably to haul the quarried stone, as well made as many manufactured today. The Egyptians were great ropemakers and rope was obviously valued by them. One of the treasures discovered by archaeologists in the tomb of Tutankhamun was a neatly coiled and braided rope.

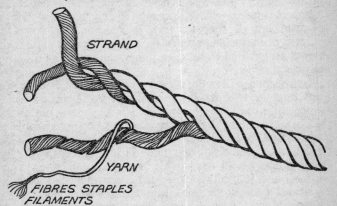

STRAND

YARN

FIBRES STAPLES FILAMENTS

Fig. 1 Rope's Construction
Right-hand, hawser-laid (3-strand) rope.

They were not the first. The Peruvian Incas made fibre ropes into primitive suspension bridges, while the North American Indians went whale hunting with 4–5″ circumference lines said to be as strong as manilla fibre but lasting four times as long in water.

Ropemaking was brought to Britain by the Romans who found the climate around Bridport very suitable for growing hemp; and in 1500 A.D. that part of Dorset still monopolised hemp growing for rope. By 1700 ropemaking had spread in the form of a cottage industry across the country, and ropewalks were also established in the naval dockyards at Chatham, Portsmouth and Devonport.

Samuel Pepys was Clerk to the Admiralty during the 1660s and his work took him often into ropewalks where he was fascinated by the spinning of large ropes. He arranged trials of strength between different sorts of line, and soon reckoned he knew all about rope . . . and the ropemakers' tricks. He cancelled at least one contract when old weak stuff disguised by tarring was offered him as new; and even ordered the whipping of a number of bargemen caught stealing the King's cordage.

HOW ROPE IS CONSTRUCTED

Discover for yourself how rope is constructed (fig. 1). Examine a short length of 3-strand rope. Hold it vertical and notice how the strands ascend upwards and to the right. The rope is 'laid' righthanded; 3-strand rope generally is. Lefthanded rope is a rarity and — in my experience — often 4-strands. 3 strands are stronger than 4. In addition, 4 or more strands (the French have a 6-strand rope) create an unfilled space running like a tunnel through the centre of the rope and this must be filled with a heart of cheap stuff.

Now uncoil one strand of your specimen piece of rope. The remaining two strands will continue to cling together, held securely by an invisible force; and there will be a clearly defined furrow into which the absent strand could be replaced with a little care.

Which way is the separated strand itself laid up? It's lefthanded, spiralling the opposite way to the whole rope. This is the vital principle of traditional ropemaking.

Opposing twist between strands and rope is what is holding those other two strands together. To replace the third strand successfully you must not only lay it neatly into the empty righthanded spiral groove but also exert a lefthanded twist as you do so.

Before trying that, separate out one of the yarns which make up the strand. Its removal will leave a spiral gap in the strand but, because there are many more yarns in a strand, replacing it perfectly is harder. Yarns are, of course, laid up righthanded, i.e. opposite to their strands.

Finally, each yarn is loosely spun from thin fibres or filaments and these are the basic units of any rope's construction. Manmade monofilaments will run the length of the line and not vary in thickness. Natural vegetable fibres can only be as long as the size of the plant which produced them allows. Such fibres, graded for size and quality, are known as 'staples' but will still have the irregularities of a natural product. It is all the projecting staple ends which make fibre rope hairy, and the lack of them which ensures a synthetic line is smooth. However, if fuzziness is desirable, then synthetic filaments can be chopped to staple lengths prior to spinning.

VEGETABLE (NATURAL) FIBRE ROPES

Primitive peoples twisted crude but very strong rope from roots, sinew or gut. The Vikings used the skin of sea mammals. Rawhide was braided into lariats (lassoes) and harness by Mexican vacqueros and American cowboys, who even laboriously wove watch chains with hair from their horses' tails. The Ancient Egyptians used papyrus (a reed from which parchment-like paper was also produced) and for thousands of years they, and their successors, commonly made rope from vegetable fibres.

Marco Polo wrote around 1271 that some Persian vessels were laid together by " . . . a kind of yarn made from coconut fibres"; and in 1620 the English explorer George Waymouth reported that Indians whaling along the coast of Maine used " . . . a rope which they make great and strong of Bark of Trees".

Vegetable fibre rope persisted with little change until the

Second World War. During all those centuries the most common fibres remained manilla, sisal, coir and hemp. Others included jute and raffia, even wool and silk.

Where ropemakers obtained their raw materials is a geography lesson: Manilla from the Philippines, Italian and Russian hemp, Sisal (named after a small port on the Yucutan peninsula of Central America) which also came from Java, Tanzania and Kenya. Coir came from the Malabar coast and Ceylon (Sri Lanka). There was Egyptian and American cotton, flax from New Zealand, esparto grass from Spain and North Africa as well as India, China, Japan and the West Indies.

When there's political upheaval, civil unrest or war, the ropemakers' sources may change. Thus the Crimean War of the mid-1800s caused the supply of Russian hemp to fail; and compelled the trade to turn from the soft and flexible fibres, exclusively used until that time, to hard Manilla hemp from the Far East. This proved superior in so many ways that it quickly became the most important cordage material . . . until 1941 when the fluctuations of World War II cut off Manilla.

Once more ropemakers were driven to seek a new solution. The answer was to be ropes from manmade materials, the biggest breakthrough in a thousand years. True, around 1831 iron wire ropes were used in the silver mines of Hungary and Austria. But, in 1860, men were still proud that a 2″ (circ.) whaleline could withstand a strain of a few hundred pounds. By 1960, nylon climbing ropes of similar size could withstand over 4,000 lbs.

Natural fibre ropes always had many disadvantages. They swelled and weakened when wet, jamming the knots tied in them and breaking more easily. They rotted, mildewed and decayed; were attacked by sun, weather and chemicals; the strength-to-weight ratio was low, making enormous circumferences and large storage spaces essential; while they could be cruel on the hands of sailors at any time but especially when they froze like spiky iron bars.

Nevertheless, there is nostalgia in the feel, smell and the evocative names of the old ropes; Italian tarred hemp (the best there was), Egyptian cotton (immaculate for rich men's yachts), brown and hairy coir from the fibrous coconut husk, and golden fuzzy sisal. Who knows, as we become increasingly concerned about depleting our world's finite resources, it might make sense one day to return to growing renewable ropemaking crops.

SYNTHETIC (MANMADE) ROPES

These days ropemakers no longer send to exotic ports for plants, but instead to the chemists for synthetic monofilaments conceived in laboratories. Nylon, Terylene (a tradename for polyester) and polypropylene are today's main rope materials. Their respective strengths can be thought of in the proportion 5:4:3. Most synthetics originate from oil but nylon — from coal — is strongest and very elastic. Its ability to absorb shock-loading by stretching makes it ideal for climbing, towing and mooring ropes. Terylene is strong too, but not as strong as nylon; nor does it stretch much, and pre-stretching during manufacture can remove even that, so it's suited for standing rigging and similar jobs where slackness could prove inconvenient or even disastrous. Polypropylene is the least strong of the trio, but it's cheaper so you can buy it thicker . . . and it floats. For lifelines and boating that last property can be useful.

Courlene is a tradename for polythene, the other main product. Often orange coloured, relatively weak and waxy to touch, it's cheap and cheerful but has its uses. Other substances can be shredded, combed and spun — even celluloid film has been made into rope. It was the short supply of vegetable fibres during the Second World War that stimulated the development of manmade ropes, at first for glider tow-ropes, parachute cords and naval use.

Today's manmade ropes are superb. Whether laid up in strands or (increasingly) plaited or braided, there is one for every purpose. There are massive mooring ropes for supertankers made of one giant plaited rope covered by an even larger plaited rope, braid over braid. Climbers' ropes combine strength, flexibility and lightness through a core of elastic filaments tightly enclosed inside a neatly woven sheath. Weavers and other craft workers can buy a variety of small cords and yarns; while for tough jobs on industrial sites, or in the garden, there are cruder and cheaper products. The ropemaker will even consider making you a special rope, e.g. a diver's lifeline which incorporates his telephone cable. Manmade ropes can even imitate the old natural fibre ropes in colour and texture and handling qualities. This combination of modern quality with traditional appeal can be important for the rope salesmen's order books.

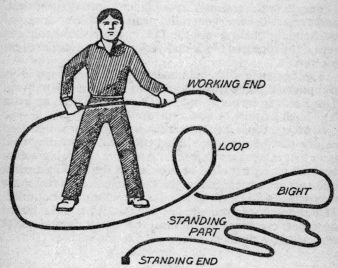

Fig. 2 Names of Rope Parts

Synthetic ropes have high tensile strength and exceptional sustained load performance; outstanding capacity to absorb shock loading; immunity to rot, mildew and marine decay. They resist chemical attack, weathering, and are also immune to degradation from contact with oils, petrol and common solvents. Because of low water absorption the breaking strain remains constant when wet (vegetable fibre strength decreases 30–40% if wet).

Manmade ropes are easy to handle, wet or dry, and their soft texture will not damage highly finished surfaces. They are lightweight, easily carried and stored, yet have a high strength-to-weight ratio. Those that float do so indefinitely, while all have excellent ageing properties, durability and long life.

Colours range from white to black, with reds, oranges, yellows, blues and greens also available. Colour coding of sheets and halyards on yachts and dinghies is now established practice in the sailing world.

Thanks to the ropemakers the fancy knotting enthusiast, and craftworkers generally, can produce work of outstanding quality; and the D.I.Y. motor mechanic can tuck a towrope and block-and-tackle into one corner of his toolbox.

The big snag with manmade rope and cordage is its smoothness. Some trusted old knots tied in it slip undone. This needs to be borne in mind. Knots may need an extra half-hitch or tuck to secure them.

Synthetic ropes also melt when heated; even the friction of one part of the rope rubbing across another may heat it so that it weakens and fails. Any sort of sawing action between rope parts must be avoided, or the binding against one another under load as the knot tightens up still more may actually fuse them all together, never again to be untied. This property of synthetic line need not be a great hazard or inconvenience, but it must be taken into account especially by climbers etc.

3
TECHNIQUES AND TERMS

The best way to learn knots is to have someone who can tie them show you how. But sooner or later most of us have to teach ourselves knotting from a book. And that's not so easy. You may be unable to follow the step-by-step drawings, or the written explanations may only confuse you. It's unfortunate but unavoidable. We all have the same difficulty. So, don't be discouraged. Persist, and you'll soon acquire the knack of working from drawings to tie real knots.

Knotting is a very big subject. Plenty of books have been written just about netting, lashings, seizing and splices, so these topics will not be touched on. It's often impractical to deal with every bit of information about one knot before passing on to another. So, having found a knot of use to you, look in the contents or illustration list and 'Knots according to Use'. There may be another mention of it elsewhere. There may be several similar knots which all do more or less the same job. It can be worth trying two or three. You might find you remember one more easily than the others. Or, in certain types of cordage, one knot may work better than the others. For this reason an effort has been made to include a number of alternatives.

TALE OF JIMMY HICKS
John Masefield, one-time Poet Laureate, wrote a hilarious salty yarn about the red-headed and ambitious Jimmy Hicks. Jimmy always tied an extra hitch on all his knots, always did more than was required of him. Ultimately, his ship and all aboard her are lost when she founders in a cyclone because Jimmy takes too long rigging a line to launch the lifeboat. The moral of this cautionary tale — enforced by generations of Royal Navy Chief Petty Officers is . . . don't you be either red-headed or ambitious, and *always use the simplest knot, bend or hitch that will serve your purpose.*

NAMES AND USES
It's no use putting lists of uses and users alongside each knot. Such lists would be long and repetitive — and would still leave people out. Instead, you should read carefully what the knot is designed for. If (say) it's a hitch to attach a rope to a rail or post or another rope, then, consider whether you need to do that at any time. It makes no difference whether you are a farmer tethering livestock or a windsurfer

securing the sail-boom to the mast. If this is the hitch for you . . . use it. (See also list of 'Knots according to Use').

Knotting isn't difficult. Certainly children can master quite complicated knots as readily as grown-ups. But — it must be said — neither is it always simple. If it was, it might not be so satisfying. You have to try, and — if it doesn't go right first time — try again.

HOW ROPE IS DESCRIBED (fig. 2)

Handling rope and tying it in knots is easier if you know what different parts of the rope are called. The 'working end' and the 'standing part' and 'standing end', 'a loop' and 'a bight' are all shown in fig. 2 and explained in the Glossary. The term 'round turn' needs explanation. When line completely encircles an object (post, rail, another rope) and the two parts of the resulting loop cross, you have "taken a turn"; but only when the end is taken round a second time is it a round turn (fig. 3). The number of 'round turns' you name is always one less than the number of rope

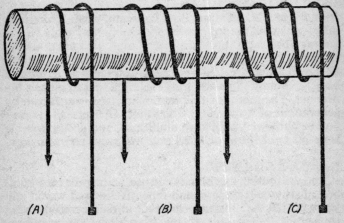

(A)　　　　　(B)　　　　　(C)

Fig. 3 Round Turns
(a) A round turn.
(b) 2 round turns.
(c) 3 round turns.

parts you see encircling the foundation.

KEY TO DRAWINGS

To help you follow the drawings you will find throughout this book that knots drawn with a single line, thick or thin, depict the working end with an arrowhead and the standing end with a black square (to signify a load, weight or strain). The exceptions are knots tied 'in the bight' (e.g. the Sheepshank fig. 21), where there is no real working end, and binding knots (e.g. the Transom Knot fig. 22) where there is no distinct load end. Drawings using a double line show the working end whipped (see Glossary).

Knot diagrams are drawn in an open layout to let you see how and where the strands cross over or under one another. The lead — i.e. the path taken by the working end — is indicated when necessary, so that you can copy the tying process. You must understand that all the knots should be tightened (see 'Tightening Knots', page 43) even though it isn't always helpful for the book to show the finished knot drawn up snug and tight with all the slack removed: however, where the finished knot takes on a totally different shape from the form in which it was tied, then that will be shown.

TOOLS

You can learn and practise knots without any tools other than your own fingers and some soft, flexible line. Two 1 metre lengths of braided white cotton rope (often called magicians' cord, or banding) or a synthetic equivalent are ideal. Climbers' or walkers' long round boot laces, obtainable from camping shops, are also perfect and can be carried in your pocket for that spare few minutes. Tying complicated knots, however, is always easier with the right implements to hand, and occasionally it can be quite impossible without one or more of the following:—

(i)   A SPIKE, to force open gaps into which working ends can be tucked, and to open tight knots. Large metal spikes are marline spikes, smaller ones with wooden handles are prickers, and wooden ones are fids;

(ii) A KNIFE, also scissors, shears, snips, pliers, nail-clippers, razor blades (in a suitable safe holder), etc., for cutting and trimming everything from a single fibre to large cables;

(iii) ROUND-BILLED PLIERS, which — used in conjunction with a thumb — will draw through slack bights when tightening knots; two pairs, one large and the other small (often called jewellers' pliers) will cope with any task.

(Spikes are readily obtained in yachting chandlery shops and everything else from a good hardware store.)

(iv) WIRE LOOPS, (fig. 4) must be homemade (you can't buy them) from piano wire bent double and inserted into suitable handles so as not to pull out in use. They are THE single most useful tool for knot tyers, used for tugging working ends through already partially tightened knots, burying ends, etc. Make several of varying lengths and a couple of thicknesses of wire.

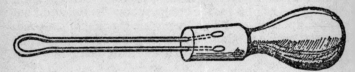

Fig. 4 A Homemade Wire Loop

HOW TO TIE A KNOT FROM A DRAWING

Take as an example a Packer's Knot (fig. 5) or Weavers' Loop Harness Knot, which will be featured later in Chapter 5, String Knots (fig. 19) and Chapter 9, parcel tying. Locate the standing end of the line in the diagram and run your eye along the line, over and under at the various crossing points (i.e. the points where line crosses line) and around the bends, until you arrive at the (arrowed) working end. This is the way you will tie it. Now take your piece of string or cord and, using about 30 centimetres (an old fashioned foot) from the working end, lay it down like the standing end of the drawing. Bend the working end around and make the first crossing point (fig. 5(B)), making sure you go over if the drawing indicates over. The over-and-under sequence must come out right. Continue to reproduce the drawing

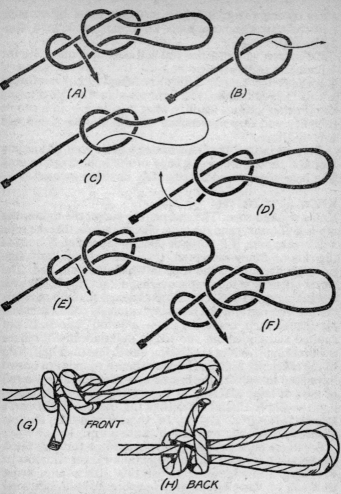

(A)

(B)

(C)

(D)

(E)

(F)

(G) FRONT

(H) BACK

Fig. 5 How to tie a knot from a drawing
(a)   Drawing of a packer's knot.
(b) – (f) Stages in tying.
(g)   Completed knot (front view).
(h)   Completed knot (rear view).

stage by stage (fig. 5(C)–(F)), crossing point by crossing
point. Draw the completed knot tight and snug (fig.
5(G)–(H)).

Of course, with practice you will develop a quick eye for
labour-saving short-cuts. You will spot that this Packer's
Knot is in fact merely a Slip Knot (fig. 19(D)) reinforced
with a Half-Hitch. So, you'll simply glance at this drawing
of a Packer's Knot, identify what it is, and — in a couple
of quick and easy movements — tie a Slip Knot and add
a Half-Hitch.

But, meantime, use the working end of your line as you
would a pencil; drawing a copy of the knot diagram until
you have reproduced it accurately in string or cord.

KNOT STRENGTH

Knots weaken rope. The sharper the curve, the tighter the
nip (see Glossary) and the more chance there is that the rope
will break; and, if it parts, it does so immediately outside
the knot. Many accepted traditional knots are sur-
prisingly harmful to the rope in which they are tied. The
worst offender is the simple overhand knot (fig. 9(A)) with
a breaking strain 40% of the rope's actual strength. Anglers
casting with rod and line can unintentionally collect it in mid
air (hence their name for it — a 'wind' knot). If not
spotted and untied but allowed to pull tight it will reduce
the breaking strain of the fishing line to less than half. Top
of the efficiency list come hitches where a round turn or two
have been taken with the line on some foundation — a rail
or spar of large diameter — before any tying takes place,
e.g. the Clove Hitch (75%) (fig. 16) and the Fisherman's
Bend (75%) (fig. 17(D)). In these knots the load is
absorbed gradually by friction in the turns.

So, knots must be chosen with care . . . a further reason
for knowing several. Climbers use bulky knots with lots of
wrapping turns devised to absorb strain and avoid
weakening nylon climbing ropes unnecessarily. Anglers use
similar (but miniature) barrel-shaped 'blood' knots in their
lines to improve their chances of a catch and prevent loss
of expensive tackle. But even the family motorist risks
something — prosecution for a dangerous or insecure load

— if the stuff on the luggage rack load comes adrift and falls into the motorway fast lane, and so also needs to know and tie good knots.

Splices are stronger than knots and, theoretically, should be used in preference to them wherever possible. Certainly don't use knots on lifting equipment such as crane slings. Splices can be 90% efficient. However, they take longer to make, are semi-permanent and so limit the rope's uses, and — if unpicked again — leave the rope forever distorted and possibly weakened as a result. Splices are not dealt with in this book but there are many excellent pamphlets by the ropemakers on splicing. Ask for one when you buy their products.

A number of modern anglers' knots are 80%, 90%, even 95% efficient; and one unique creation — the Bimini Twist (see fig. 41) is claimed to be 100% . . .as strong as the untied line.

KNOT SECURITY

Knots which perform well when steadily loaded — strong knots — may quickly slip, capsize, or fall apart when subjected to intermittent jerking; in which case, although strong, they are 'insecure'. *Strength and security are two different and quite separate considerations.*

A Double Sheet Bend (fig. 14(C)–(D)) may be no stronger than the common Sheet Bend (fig. 14(A)), but it is definitely more secure and should be used when security is essential. The common Sheet Bend is also about equal in strength with the so-called 'lefthanded' version of the knot (i.e. when the short ends finish on opposite sides), but the lefthanded Sheet Bend is significantly less *secure* which is why the correct method of tying it with both short ends on the same side is stressed in this book.

Selecting the best knot for the job is clearly a fine art; but it is NOT yet a precise science. We really know very little about what goes on inside a knot. Testing and measuring knot performance could be a fascinating pastime and a fruitful field of research for someone.

Where there is general agreement about a knot's breaking strength, it's placed in brackets following that knot's name.

ROPE STRENGTH

An extraordinary tug-o'-war in the U.S.A. a couple of years ago ended in mishap when the 1½" thick nylon rope snapped, injuring dozens of the 2,200 participants! The wonder is that it actually stood the strain for 12 minutes before parting. For, although the minimum breaking load of the rope was no doubt believed more than enough by the organisers, the surging momentum of so many straining people would make nonsense of any normal prediction.

Whether you must moor a super-tanker to an oil rig, or just fit a curtain pull to your venetian blind, the ropemakers can supply you with detailed performance specifications for their products, including safe working loads. If in doubt, choose line with a much greater minimum breaking load than is strictly necessary. Lifeboat falls (the ropes which lower them into the water) are required to be six times as strong as actually needed to do the job.

Vegetable fibre ropes are weaker than manmade ones; and, oddly, new natural fibre ropes can be weaker than those made years ago. Vegetable fibre is only half as strong when wet; and it has a low strength-to-weight ratio. Greater strength is obtained only by resorting to much larger circumferences (24" diameter cables were not unknown in Nelson's time).

By comparison, manmade ropes are so strong and light that it is frequently necessary to use line many times stronger than needed, just to have something large enough to grip comfortably. Synthetic line does not absorb water and the breaking strain remains constant when wet.

Synthetic line has one major drawback; it deteriorates rapidly at high temperatures and melts at the following points: nylon — 250°C, polyester — 260°C, polypropylene — 165°C. You will be reminded of this fact later.

Rope is expensive. Care will prolong its life and preserve its strength to ensure you get your money's worth. Any misuse, such as dragging it over sharp or rough edges, or over surfaces where abrading particles of dirt and grit can penetrate between strands and yarns, will nick large numbers of individual fibres. The result will be a weaker rope, the effect being greater on small sizes of rope than on larger ones. Inspect it periodically, and wash out dirt and grit. Avoid stepping on rope, or forcing it into harsh kinks. Rope slung over hooks to lift loads, or just tied around a car towing eye, will be weakened by as much as 30%.

Curiously, 4-strand rope is 11% weaker than 3-strand equivalent; and cable-laid line (three 3-strand ropes laid up lefthanded to form a 9-strand cable) is 40% weaker than the same size of hawser-laid (ordinary 3-strand) rope.

Old-time sailormen referred to rope size by its circumference in inches; and they estimated breaking strain by squaring the circumference and then dividing the product by any number from 2 to 12, depending upon the kind of rope and experience, to arrive at a breaking load in tons. You can still find these methods in print. Today, rope performance can be predicted with greater accuracy from formulae and graphs. It's no longer sold by the fathom (6 feet lengths) but by the metre, and its size is the DIAMETER measured in millimetres (roughly 25mm. to 1 inch).

UNTYING KNOTS

Generally knots should be untied again after use, and this will be easier if you choose a suitable one in the first place. Select a knot — if possible — which cannot jam and is easily undone, e.g. the Lighterman's Back Mooring Hitch (fig. 37) which will hold a tow of 6 laden barges whose combined weight is hundreds of tonnes, yet which takes only seconds to cast loose in an emergency. The Timber Hitch (fig. 18) is another such knot. Use knots which disappear when slipped off their foundations, e.g. the Clove Hitch (fig. 16), a Scaffold Hitch (fig. 16(C)) and the Prusik Knot (fig. 61). Add a draw-loop. The knots will be no less strong or secure, but you can then undo them with a single tug, e.g. the Sheet Bend may be modified in this way (fig. 14(E)), while the Highwayman's Hitch (fig. 38) is nothing but a succession of draw-loops. Find out which knots capsize into a different form and can then be slid apart, e.g. the Reef Knot (fig. 12), the Sheet Bend (fig. 14) and the Bowline (fig. 13). Reduce knots to simpler forms, e.g. the Fisherman's Knot (fig. 15), the two halves of which may be separated and each part untied on its own. Don't break fingernails. Stubborn knots can be poked and prised apart with a spike.

Occasionally it may be necessary to cut line. *Never hesitate if it will prevent or reduce loss or harm to someone.* Suppose you are a first-aider or an early arrival at the scene of violent crime; and you are confronted with the need to release a trussed-up hostage or victim of strangulation. Summon up your courage. Insert two fingers between the line and the victim's flesh; then, using the gap so obtained, cut away from the person. Do NOT sever any knot, which should be preserved for forensic examination and a Coroner's inquest.

UNTANGLING LINE

No matter how methodically you stow away line, when next you go to use it, it looks like a bird's nest. To sort out such a muddle there is an effective trick. Firstly, keep the tangle as loose as possible; do NOT pull experimentally or impatiently until the whole lot jams up. Locate the point where the end enters the tangle. Enlarge the aperture around it, arranging the tangle to resemble a ring doughnut. Rotate this 'ring' outwards so that the lengthening end of the rope continues to emerge from the centre of the mess. This gimmick often works and is always worth a try. During my time as a swimming coach I always managed to untangle pool lane ropes this way, and they had the added obstructions of floats attached every couple of metres. If the rope is too snarled up for this method, there is no alternative but the laborious process of pulling the loose end through repeatedly.

constrictor knot (fig. 6)

One knot has emerged in the last few years, its history obscure, to be recognised belatedly as very special. It is the Constrictor Knot, which consists of a simple or overhand knot trapped beneath a diagonal round turn (fig. 6(A)) which acts just like a retaining finger to hold it secure. I cannot recommend it too highly. If you want a knot that will grip tightly and stay tied, learn this one.

Use it as a temporary or semi-permanent whipping on ropes' ends; instead of a vice or clamp to hold newly glued items together while they dry; on the joints of hosepipes;

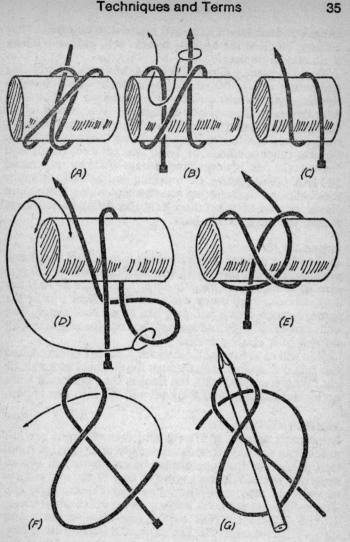

(A)

(B)

(C)

(D)

(E)

(F)

(G)

Fig. 6 Constrictor Knot

in the construction of kites and models; to improvise rope
ladders; to close the neck of a sack; etc., etc., etc. There
is no end to its uses.

To tie it, make a Clove Hitch and then tuck the working
end once more (fig. 6(B)) to form the overhand knot beneath
the diagonal. A really quick way — which can only be done
near the end of the rope or whatever — is to take a round
turn (fig. 6(C)), and pull out a bight which is then partially
un-twisted (fig. 6(D)) as it is passed over the end (fig. 6(E)).
Several other methods of tying can be discovered; and
perhaps the best is a one-handed way. Write an ampersand
(&) (fig. 6(F)), passing the working end behind the upper
loop. Pick up the resulting arrangement with a thumb and
finger. or pass an object through it, (fig. 6(G)), to transform
it into the recognisable knot.

important tip
*If the object around which the knot is to be tied is soft and
yielding (e.g. another rope), use hard cord which will bite
into it. If the object itself is hard (like a pipe or rail) use
soft, stretchy stuff to tie the knot.* The effect will be the
same. In each case it will grip like a boa constrictor. The
ends can be cut off close against the knot for neatness with
no risk of it coming adrift.

You will have to cut a Constrictor Knot off after use; and
this is best done by slicing through the diagonal with a single
cut. Whatever is beneath the knot is thus protected from
accidental damage, and the knot will fall into two halves.

WHIPPINGS (fig. 7)
Rope costs money. If it's cut and then the ends are left
unseized in any way, strands will unravel and yarns fray until
that portion of the rope cannot be reconstructed. It's an
expensive waste. Whipping prevents fraying and also ensures
ropes' ends pass easily through pulley blocks, eyes, etc.
Three different methods will cope with all circumstances.
1. The CONSTRICTOR KNOT (fig. 6) — a quick and
highly effective seizing; 2. The COMMON WHIPPING (fig.
7(A)—(C)) — a neat and secure, permanent treatment for
ropes' ends which is easy to apply and has been used for

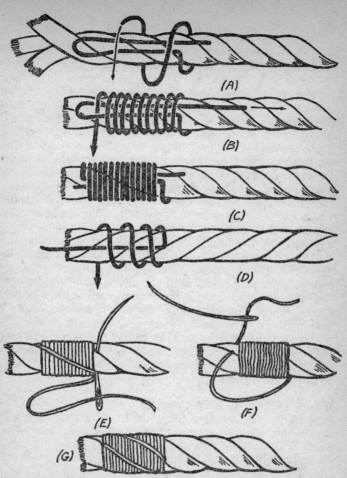

(A)

(B)

(C)

(D)

(E)

(F)

(G)

Fig. 7 Whipping – common, and Palm and Needle
Common whipping:
(a) Make a bight in the standing end and wrap it tightly against the rope as shown.
(b) Tuck the working end through the bight.
(c) Pull firmly on the standing end to trap the working end beneath the turns of the whipping. Trim both ends short.
(d)–(g) Palm and Needle Whipping – see text.

centuries; 3. A PALM-AND-NEEDLE WHIPPING (fig. 7(D)–(G)) — after applying wrapping turns like any other whipping (fig. 7(D)), riding turns are created. On an ordinary hawser-laid (i.e. 3-strand) rope there will be 3 riding turns, one resting in each groove between strands; and they are made by simply stitching the working end of twine through each strand in turn with a needle (fig. 7(E)–(G)) as it snakes backwards and forwards from one end of the whipping to the other. Start at the outside end and to finish off stitch the end of your whipping twine back and forth across the body of the rope a couple of times. A palm-and-needle whipping should never come off, even though the rope's end is flogging about in a wind; and it can be applied just as well to braided or sheath-and-core lines.

Always bind AGAINST the lay of the strands so that any tendency for the line to open under load will automatically tighten your whipping. Use vegetable fibre twine on vegetable fibre rope, and synthetic thread on synthetic rope. Start the binding process away from the end of the rope and work towards it, trimming the end afterwards to within 7 or 8 mm. of the whipping. How near depends on the size of the rope. Whippings need to be as long as the width of the rope, i.e. square to look at, or just a trifle longer. A real 'belt-and-braces' job will result if you also paint, varnish or glue your whippings.

HEAT SEALING ENDS (fig. 8)

When a flame is applied to synthetic yarns they melt and shrink away, leaving a small globule of molten material on

(A)   *(B)*   *(C)*

Fig. 8 Heat Sealed Ends

the fibre ends. This quickly cools and congeals. To seal ropes' ends this way is lazy and can be dangerous. I once saw a Thames tugman with the palm of his hand sliced open to the sinews after the hardened (and obviously sharp) end of a hawser — unwhipped but heat sealed — had been pulled through his grasp. There is no substitute for a properly made whipping.

Rope stockists measure out the line they sell and sever it by means of an electrically heated guillotine which does a neat job without the ugly, oversized gob of hardened plastic which can inflict wounds. So, melting ends can still be a quick and labour saving trick of the trade. To fit a small pull-cord to a ceiling light switch in the bathroom, deliberately create a mushroom shaped bulb (fig. 8(A)) in one end (instead of a stopper knot) to retain the line within the fitting. Fancy knotting and macramé enthusiasts who work with dozens, even hundreds, of strands need not bother to whip each one. Just touch them briefly on a cherry red cooker element or a blue gas flame for a normal seal (fig. 8(B)). If you wet your fingertips first, you may even pinch the melted ends to points (fig. 8(C)) for easier threading of beads. (CAUTION — Pinching hot ends of line is similar to snuffing out candles by hand or touching a smoothing iron to see if it's hot enough; if you're quick, it's all right . . . but you can burn your fingers, especially if the molten material sticks to your skin.)

OTHER METHODS WITH ENDS

Some boat chandlers sell a special pair of pliers which apply expanded collars to ropes' ends. This ingenious device, together with a supply of the right sized rubber collars, can be a very useful first aid kit for anyone handling ropes. A roll of adhesive tape is almost as good. Neither however can replace the longer lasting, more attractive, traditional whipping.

STOPPER KNOTS (figs. 9–10)

A stopper knot stops the end of rope, cord or smaller stuff coming out of a hole. Needlewomen tie a stopper knot in cotton to prevent it pulling through material. Building

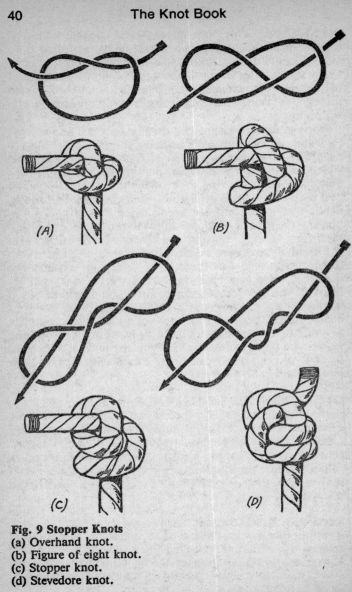

Fig. 9 Stopper Knots
(a) Overhand knot.
(b) Figure of eight knot.
(c) Stopper knot.
(d) Stevedore knot.

workers tie one in the rope which passes through a pulley block to stop it unreeving. A stopper knot can be used (instead of heat-sealing) to fix that bathroom light-pull, or to re-string a musical instrument. All the stopper knots shown build from a Simple, Overhand or Thumb Knot (fig. 9(A)), which is the simplest variety. The FIGURE OF EIGHT KNOT (fig. 9(B)) (so called because of its outline, but also known as the 'Flemish Knot') starts as if to tie an Overhand Knot but the loop is given half a twist before the end is tucked through it. The STOPPER KNOT (fig. 9(C)) starts as a Figure of Eight Knot but an extra half twist is made before the end is tucked; while the STEVEDORE KNOT (fig. 9(D)) is a Stopper Knot with an extra half twist before tucking.

Note that all stopper knots pulled tight are unlike their flattened out diagrams. The pull is on the standing part only, dragging down the short end until it projects more or less at right angles to the line. The end is trapped within a top bight, while the body of the knot winds into a collar around the body of the rope, forming the stopper. Don't use stopper knots instead of whippings, except in very small twines.

An Overhand Knot enlarged by tucking the working end through its own loop 2, 3, 4 or more times becomes a DOUBLE OVERHAND KNOT (fig. 10(A)), a TRIPLE OVERHAND KNOT (fig. 10(B)), etc; and all of these multiple overhand knots are known as 'Blood Knots'. The name comes from their use by surgeons for tying off severed blood vessels, or perhaps because they are found in the lashes of particularly cruel whips for flogging people.

There is a special technique for tying them. Do NOT just pull on both ends of the line. Instead, keep the knot open and loose, pull very gently on each end and at the same time steadily twist the two ends of line in opposite directions. You'll soon discover which way to twist. If you go the wrong way, nothing much will happen. Going the right way will cause the knot itself to twist and adopt a form with the loop wrapping itself in a spiral around the knot. Master this method. Quite a few other knots you will meet later are tied the same way. Continue to work the knot tighter and snugger — but sympathetically — permitting the knot to settle itself

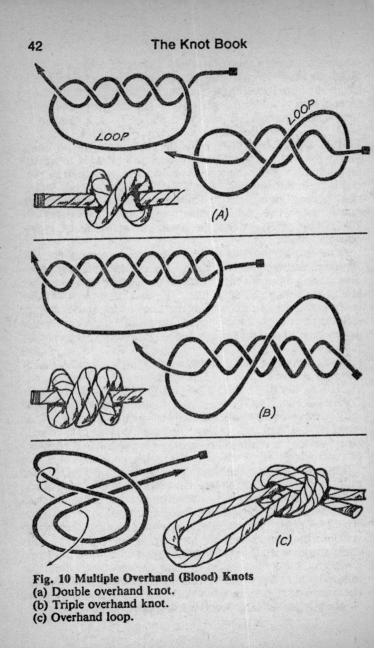

LOOP

LOOP

(A)

(B)

(C)

Fig. 10 Multiple Overhand (Blood) Knots
(a) Double overhand knot.
(b) Triple overhand knot.
(c) Overhand loop.

the way it wants to go. The OVERHAND LOOP KNOT (fig. 10(C)) is an overhand knot said to be "tied in the bight". It makes a somewhat clumsy stopper knot but the extra bulk proves invaluable to retain the strings of some musical instruments.

TIGHTENING KNOTS
Working up stopper knots makes you recognise the principles of tightening any knot. 1. You must know what the finished knot looks like. 2. Newly tied knots need to be encouraged in the direction of the finished form by patient pushing. 3. Next, tighten them by gradually removing slack from each part of the knot in turn, a little at a time. 4. *Never distort the knot beyond recognition by just tugging on both ends. Very few knots can be tightened by pulling the two ends.* Even the Reef Knot (fig. 12) has 4 parts emerging from the knot, and each should be gently pulled in turn to ensure the knot settles down evenly. 5. Knotted rope or cord knows which way it wants to lie. You can't force it to do differently. E.g. the Figure of Eight stopper knot (fig. 9(B)) will always have its end askew. If it's important for it to be fairly straight, pick another knot (say, the Double Overhand Knot) (fig. 10(A)).

KNOTS, BENDS AND HITCHES (DEFINITIONS)
A KNOT is only a knot, strictly speaking, when tied in the end of line as a stopper, or forming a loop or noose, or in two ends of the same piece of line used to parcel or bind (e.g. the Constrictor Knot, fig. 6). However, the term 'knot' is also used when two pieces of very small stuff are tied together, e.g. anglers' monofilaments. A BEND (e.g. the Full Carrick Bend, fig. 29) joins two free lines together and so one rope is said to be "bent to" another. A HITCH (e.g. the Round Turn & Two Half Hitches, fig. 17) secures a line to a post, ring or spar, or to another rope which takes no part in the actual knotting.

Bends generally unite ropes of *equal* thickness. Certain bends will cope with lines of very different sizes (e.g. the sheet bend, full carrick bend, bowline bend, heaving line bend) and, where these bends occur in this book, the fact is mentioned or obvious from the illustrations.

To hitch the working end of one line onto the standing part of another, when the two lines differ in size, always assume the thinner one forms the hitch around the thicker one. It is just about impossible to make a secure hitch with thick cordage around a small diameter.

LAYING UP STRANDS BY HAND

Neglected rope — and you see it everywhere, unwhipped and unravelled — is an expensive waste. It shouldn't be allowed to get to that state. Before re-whipping it, try to avoid cutting off the unravelled section by laying up the strands again. It may be possible to put them back together again, although extremely tight-laid line (done by machine, remember) can never be quite the same when re-laid by hand.

Use your knowledge of twist and countertwist to reproduce the lost section of rope. Spread and hold the 3 strands between the forefinger and thumb of one hand, curling the remaining three fingers around the body of the rope itself. Impart a strong lefthanded twist (i.e. anticlockwise as you look at the end of the strand) with your other hand to the uppermost strand so as to tighten still further its lefthanded lay; then immediately pull it over and down behind the other two strands, trapping it there.

What was the middle strand has now emerged on top. Continue to twist and then re-lay each strand as it becomes the top one, drawing the completed rope a centimetre at a time through your gripping hand with your spare fingers. Finally, whip your handiwork (fig. 7).

Using this technique you can actually make up short lengths of your own cordage using any sort of small stuff, and any combination of colours. Taking thin and comparatively weak threads or cords, you can produce an original, thicker and stronger product. Most satisfying.

SWIGGING (fig. 11)

This is the only name I know for this trick. I learned it sailing Whalers in Christchurch Harbour as a boy. If the mains'l had even one small wrinkle in it the grizzled old sailing master would want the main halyard hauled down tighter but it would be straining so much already that just pulling

Fig. 11 Swigging

on it would gain nothing. In fact, once cast loose, it would snatch back and you'd lose more than you'd tried to gain. "Swig the blighter up" he'd growl, and he'd be right. Do not let the line go completely from its belaying point (for example the cleat where it is made fast). Leave at least a ½ turn (fig. 11(A)) around some robust anchorage. The friction gained will enable you to hang onto what you've got. Then, holding this ½ turn firm with one hand, grasp the standing part with the other and pull it out of line (fig. 11(B)) like a bowstring. The leverage is so great you'll always be able to gain some slack this way. The next stage is where you win over the rope . . . but you must be quick. Let the bent rope go with a twang, just as if you were releasing a bowstring (fig. 11(C)), but at the same moment pull in on the other hand. You'll gain some extra centimetres of line which you then hold via the friction of the ½ turn. Repeat the process rhythmically — heave in, release and pull — several times. It'll be a fight and the rope will creak alarmingly but that's the way to do it. Finally make fast. This is a useful technique to tighten up loads on car luggage racks, for raising flags and even for parcel tying.

FORMING LOOPS

This way of manipulating lines can make your knot tying skilful. It can be used to help tie several knots, especially when the rope is already under a moderate amount of strain and there is little or no slack available in the standing part e.g. the Bowline (see fig. 13(G)–(H)) and the Sheepshank (see fig. 21(E)–(F)). Make a half hitch (fig. 13(G)). Now pull the working end of the line in the direction of the arrow until it springs straight. You will find that the standing part now forms a loop around the working end instead. Pull that part straight, removing the loop, and it will reappear in the first part.

4
BASIC KNOTS

Those whose work involves rope all use the same few basic knots. During my 10 years working afloat on the commercial Thames tideway, I saw watermen, lightermen, merchant seamen of many nations, river police, harbour masters and customs and excise crews tying knots. They had all settled for the same ones, which they used to moor ships, shift heavy cargoes, and every possible job from hanging out their washing to recovering dead and decomposing corpses. Knots trusted by these hardy professionals clearly merit everybody's attention. There were 7 and they were:— *2 knots,* the Reef Knot (fig. 12) and the Bowline (fig. 13); *2 bends* — the Sheet Bend (fig. 14) and the Fisherman's Knot (fig.15) (yes, it's a bend, see p.43); and *3 hitches* — the Clove Hitch (fig. 16), the Round Turn & Two Half Hitches (fig. 17), and the Timber Hitch (fig. 18). They've certain good features in common. They're easy to learn and tie. Each has a distinctive appearance, so you know when you've got it right. They can be easily untied and cast off; and re-tied in line repeatedly without ruining it. It's even possible to tie them one-handed and that can be vital. "Use one hand for the job . . . keep the other for yourself" (in other words "hang on"). That advice is drilled into every young apprentice afloat. It's just as applicable to rock climbers or window cleaners or forestry workers.

reef knot (breaking strain 45%) (fig. 12)
The Reef Knot is flat and symmetrical (fig. 12(A)), consisting of two interlocked bights with both short ends on the same side. If it isn't flat it's a Granny Knot. If the ends are on opposite sides it's a Thief Knot, as in fig. 86 and on the front cover. Neither is as strong nor as secure. So tie it by placing one Overhand Knot on top of another, taking care that one of the knots is lefthanded and the other righthanded. Remember; "Tie left over right; then, right over left" (fig. 12(B)–(D)).

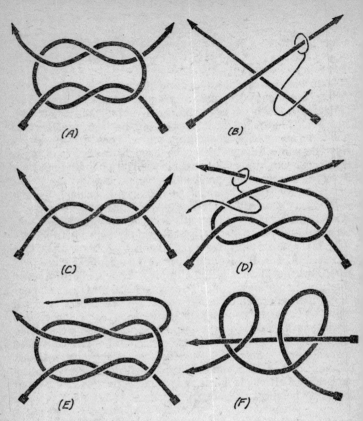

(A)

(B)

(C)

(D)

(E)

(F)

Fig. 12 Reef Knot

Reef Knots may be quickly freed by pulling sharply (fig. 12(E)) on one end. This capsized version is a Lark's Head Knot (fig. 12(F)) which may be slid apart fairly easily. Releasing the Reef Knot is easier still if, as you tie it, you leave one end only partly drawn through to form a quick release draw-loop. This makes a Single Reef Bow. When both ends form draw-loops (e.g. like tying shoe laces) it's a Double Reef Bow. That is, sadly, the only knot most parents ever teach their children. Incidentally, just as many people unknowingly tie a Granny Knot, so many use a Double Granny Bow on their shoes; and this will work loose more often than a Double Reef Bow. People who just accept that it's routine to re-tie shoe laces several times a day are probably not using the Double Reef Bow.

The Reef Knot must NEVER be used as a BEND. It is strictly a KNOT, used to parcel or bind by tying the two ends of the same piece of line. This way the actual knot presses against whatever it is securing. It is ideal for bandages and slings, head scarves, etc. Don't use it to join pieces of rope, nor on two lines of differing diameters. It could slip or jam and either way it's unreliable.

The Reef Knot is an ancient knot. Late Stone Age folk knew the differences between a Reef Knot and a Granny Knot. Greeks and Romans called it the Hercules Knot. The ease with which it can be spilled to form a Lark's Head Knot and then slipped apart made it perfect for reefing sails . . . hence Reef Knot. Americans know it as the Square Knot, not to be confused with the Square Knot (fig. 27) we'll learn later.

bowline (b.s. — 60%) (fig. 13)

The Bowline (say "Boh-linn") (fig. 13(A)) forms a loop that will not slip in a single end of line. The lefthanded Bowline (fig. 13(B)) is less secure, so don't use it. To tie the common Bowline first form a loop in the standing part of the line as shown. Next, pass the working end up (fig. 13(C)) through the eye of the loop, around the back of the standing part, and then back down through the eye once more. Practise until you can tie it fast, with your eyes closed.

It's a simple, strong and secure knot which holds tight the greater the strain placed upon it, yet can always be untied easily by pushing forward the bight which encircles the standing part of the line. Use it for climbing, lifesaving and boating, and in the end of parcel string. The Running Bowline (fig. 13(D)) makes a noose which readily falls open once tension comes off it. The Bowline Bend (fig. 13(E)) joins large less manageable hawsers or cables temporarily, just as illustrated, with two common Bowlines interlocked.

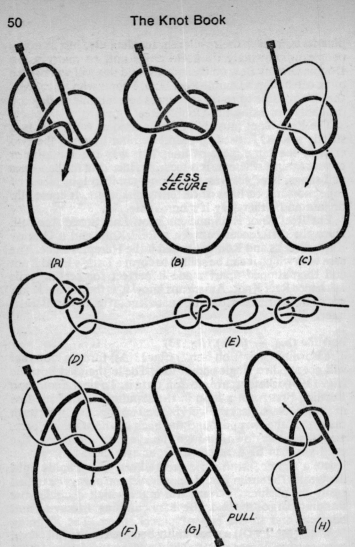

LESS SECURE

(A) (B) (C)

(D) (E)

(F) (G) PULL (H)

Fig. 13 Bowline
(g) – (h) Tying a Bowline upside down by forming a loop in the working end and transferring it to the standing part.

The ropes may each be a different thickness.

A word of caution — the Bowline may be a little less reliable in modern synthetic ropes. If so, secure the end with an extra half-hitch, or tuck it and trap it beneath one of the rope's strands.

A more secure version of the Bowline called the Double Bowline (fig. 13(F)) should be tied if the knot is likely to be towed over rough ground or through water.

If you ever have to tie a Bowline speedily and snugly under the armpits of some poor soul in distress down a cliff face or overboard from a boat, you will quickly realise — too late — that it takes practice to tie the knot when you are looking at it from the wrong direction! Spend time now learning to tie it 'upside down' (fig. 13(G)–(H)). See also Forming Loops, page 46.

sheet bend (b.s. — 50%) (fig. 14)

The Sheet Bend (fig.14(A)) has the same layout as a Bowline (fig. 13) but the strain comes differently upon it. It's used for joining two lines together. They may be of slightly different diameters but too great a difference in thickness between the two lines would make the bend most insecure and should be avoided.

To tie it, form a bight in one line (and, if the lines are dissimilar, the bight is always formed in the thicker one). Pass the working end of the other (thinner) line up through the eye formed, around the back and trap it in place under its own standing part (fig. 14(B)). Take care not to go back down through the bight. Note that both short ends finish up on the same side.

If the bight is made in stiffish stuff it has a tendency to open up, which may be counteracted by a second turn around the neck of the bight with the working end. This results in a Double Sheet Bend (fig. 14(C)–(D)). In either knot a draw-loop (fig. 14(E)) may be left as a quick-release device.

The Sheet Bend is a good utility bend which can withstand a great strain yet undoes readily afterwards, even without a draw-loop, by rolling forward the bight encircling the single line. Should the knot be tied with short ends on opposite sides, this is a lefthanded Sheet Bend which is less

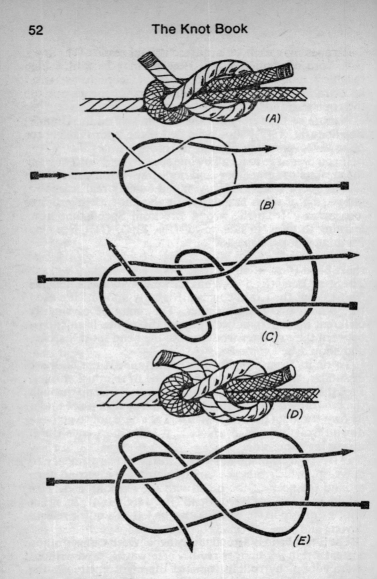

Fig. 14 Sheet Bend.

secure and so should be avoided. The principle of the Sheet Bend can be adapted to make fast a line to anything which has an aperture through which a single line may be passed and trapped beneath itself, e.g. the handle of a spade or other implement to be lifted or hung by a rope.

The Sheet Bend appeared in Ancient Egyptian art but the name first appeared in print in 1794 because it secured ropes (known in nautical circles as 'sheets') to sails. Before that it had a number of other names, the most usual being 'Common Bend' (still reproduced in some books) and 'Swab Hitch' (which I saw recently on a tea towel with a diagram of the knot) when it was used to attach rope handles to mops.

fisherman's knot (b.s. — 65%) (fig. 15)

The Fisherman's Knot (fig.15(A)) is a compact arrangement of two overhand knots embedded one against the other, with short ends on opposite sides and lying almost parallel to their nearest standing part.

Tie it by positioning the two lines alongside one another facing opposite directions. Tie an overhand knot with one end (fig. 15(B)) so as to enclose and grip the standing part of the other line. Reverse the lines and make an IDENTICAL overhand knot with the other end enclosing its nearby standing part. Pull the two knots together.

Use it for joining lines of equal thickness. Climbers use it. So do anglers. It is equally well suited for small stuff or rope, but generally recommended for small cord and twines (the sharp curves might be too harsh for big hawsers).

Tie a double (fig. 15(C)) or triple overhand knot in each end and you have a Double (fig. 15(D)) or Triple Fisherman's Knot, which is thought to be stronger. *Note:* there's another knot (fig. 17(D)) called a Fisherman's Bend, although it's a hitch! Don't confuse the two.

The Fisherman's Knot is actually a BEND, relatively strong and suited to small cordage. Because the Fisherman's Knot is tied in small stuff it is called a 'knot' (see definition p.43). Curiously, while some writers strongly recommend it, others ignore it. Seamanship manuals mostly omit it, perhaps because of the prejudice against using it in large sizes of rope. The only time I tied it in two hawsers I had to cut it out with an axe, it jammed so firmly. Yet some authorities claim it is easily loosened, even in large rope.

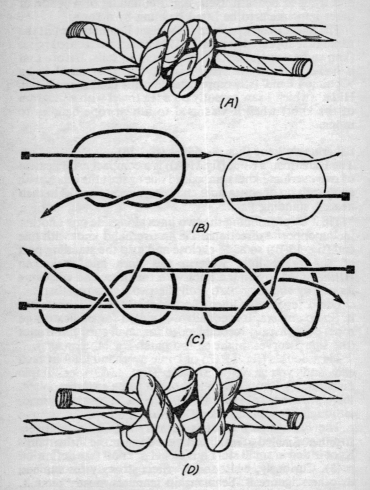

(A)

(B)

(C)

(D)

Fig. 15 Fisherman's Knot

Normally, it can be pulled apart and the two overhand knots dealt with separately.

Another knot known to the Ancient Greeks, this one has picked up more names than most over the centuries . . . and will still be located in some books as the Englishman's Bend, Halibut Knot, True Lover's Knot or Bend, Water Knot, Waterman's Knot and Angler's Knot.

clove hitch (b.s. — 75%) (fig. 16)

The front view of a Clove Hitch (fig. 16(A)) resembles a letter 'N' (although, as the diagonal part may go either way it may be written backwards).

The Clove Hitch is used to fasten a line to a rail, post or bollard, or onto another rope which is not part of the knot but only if the strain will remain steady and at right-angles. It can be used to hang things in your garage, or scenery backstage or to suspend a fender from a boat but it is not a very secure mooring hitch although it's often used. Distorted (fig. 16(B)), it makes a safe scaffold hitch (fig. 16(C)) to support a workman's plank seat.

Tying the Clove Hitch is quick and easy, and it is notable for the many different ways it can be tied. Basically, pass the working end around the hitching rail, cross the standing part at the front, take another trip around in the same direction, and finally trap the end beneath the diagonal. But, should the end of the line be inaccessible (or simply for speed) form two opposing loops (fig. 16(D)), cross the loops placing the 2nd one on top of the 1st and slip the result over the post (fig. 16(E)), etc. Alternatively, on a vertical post, apply an underhand loop (fig. 16(F)), using this frictional device to slow and stop the load on the line; then lock in place with a second half hitch (fig. 16(G)) similarly applied. Forming the loops in large sizes of rope is best done while it is lying on the ground or deck — either with one hand or a docker's hook — and then the two can be picked up together. Small cord can, with a little ingenuity, be tied one-handed.

The Clove Hitch is one of the most valuable hitches, provided the strain always comes from the same direction. Otherwise, it quickly works loose. Slip it off the end of the

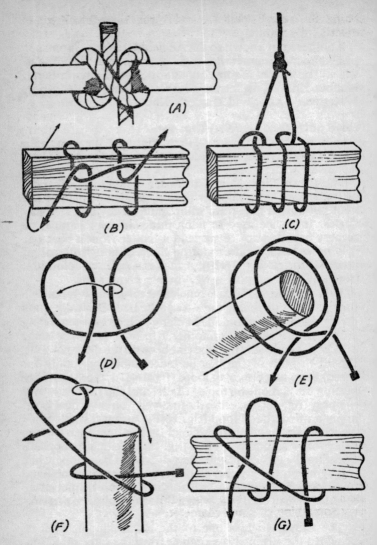

Fig. 16 Clove Hitch

spar around which it was tied and it just falls apart. If great strain is to be applied, and the diameter is small, use a draw-loop (fig. 16(G)).

The name Clove Hitch was first used in Falconer's 'Dictionary of the Marine' in 1796. Samuel Pepys knew Falconer — and also knew about knots — so he probably knew the Clove Hitch. In 1884 the knotting authority Burgess wrote that the Clove Hitch could be ". . . made in the bight as if it was a single piece of line, this tie is often used by surgeons in cases of dislocation of the thumb." (Ouch!)

round turn & two half hitches (b.s. — 70%) (fig. 17)

The name describes exactly what this knot looks like; a round turn (refer to fig. 3 if you need to) secured by two hitches, one beneath the other (fig. 17(A)).

Use it any time you need to attach a line securely to a beam, rail, pole, ring, hook or handle. It moors boats safely and will support loads of any description. It's a real all-rounder.

To tie it, take the working end around the securing point to make a round turn, (fig. 17(B)), slowing and holding the load — whatever it is — by friction. Secure with two half hitches (fig. 17(C)) worked up snugly against each other and the first part of the knot. For extra security, especially if the line is likely to be wet or slippery, pass the first half-hitch THROUGH the round turn. This forms a Fisherman's Bend (fig.17(D)) (B.S. — 75%) (which is NOT, of course, a bend at all; it's a hitch). Don't be tempted to use the Fisherman's Bend instead of the Round Turn & Two Half Hitches for everything. With a load on it you may be unable to free it when you need to . . . remember Jimmy Hicks! (See Chapter 3 — Techniques and Terms.)

The Round Turn & Two Half Hitches is the most generally used one of a number of such hitches. It is a strong and secure old hold-fast which never jams and is good when tied over something of small diameter.

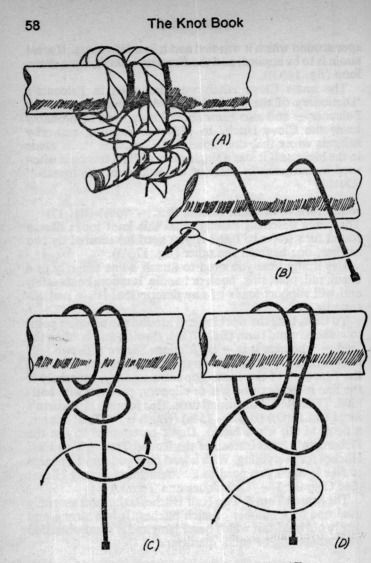

Fig. 17 Round Turn & Two Half Hitches (A) – (C),
(D) Fisherman's Bend.

timber hitch (b.s. — 70%) (fig. 18)

The Timber Hitch (fig. 18(A)) is a temporary noose made by doubling the working end back on itself and wrapping (or 'dogging') it around its own standing part (fig. 16(B)–(C)) several times. Clearly, this only works if the noose remains firmly around some object. Often there is a half-hitch added some distance from the original knot; and the arrangement is then called a 'Killick Hitch' (fig. 18(D)). The appearance of a Timber (or Killick) Hitch is unmistakeable.

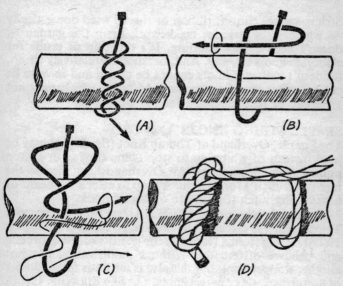

Fig. 18 Timber Hitch
(a) – (c) Timber Hitch.
(d)   Killick Hitch

Use it for towing, dragging, lifting or lowering through water, over land or in air, logs, planks, poles, piling, scaffolding or anything else which is long and relatively thin.

5
STRING

> "String
> Is a very important thing,
> Rope is thicker,
> But string is quicker."
>
> (Spike Milligan)

String, twine, cotton, ribbon or thread used domestically — whether for parcels, needlework or in the garden — doesn't need expert knotting. It's too thin or crude for elaborate knots anyway. And, because it's relatively cheap, it doesn't matter if knots cannot be untied and have to be cut off after use. So you can use knots which may not generally be recommended for use with rope.

SIMPLE STRING KNOTS AND USES

The Simple, Overhand or Thumb Knot (fig. 19(A)) may be used instead of whipping to stop twine fraying or cotton pulling through material. An Overhand Knot tied in the bight (fig. 19(B)) forms a quick loop to attach by means of a bale sling hitch (fig. 39) to a ring or hook.

The simple Noose (fig. 19(C)) is a start for tying parcels. Tying parcels is discussed in chapter 9. The Slip Knot (fig. 19(D)) differs from a Noose by the position of its short end and behaves differently. Without modification it's just another stopper knot; but this also is the basis for a number of useful packer's or parcel knots. The Slip Knot (fig. 19(E)), its short end stopped with an Overhand Knot, is a further alternative for starting parcels while another packer's knot (fig. 19(F)) uses a Slip Knot but this time the end is locked by a half-hitch. Fig. 19(G) shows another variation of a packer's knot.

The Overhand Knot can also be tied in the ends of two parallel strands (fig. 19(H)), such as a needlewoman's doubled thread. Or, it can act as a collection knot (fig. 19(I)) gathering together several strands to form a fringe or tassel. The Water Knot (fig. 19(J)) is an overhand bend.

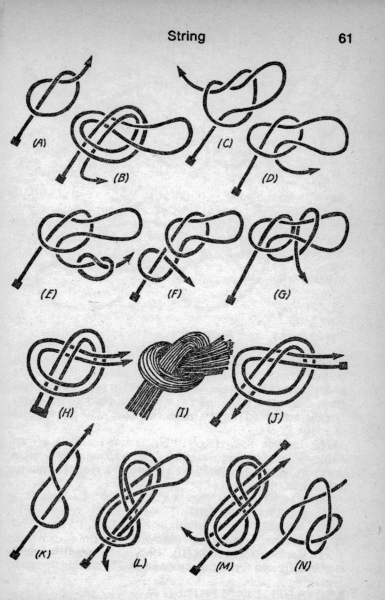

Fig. 19 String Knots

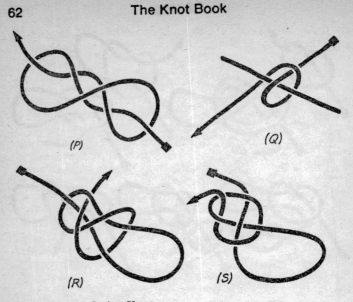

Fig. 19 (cont.) String Knots

The Figure of Eight Knot (fig. 19(K)) is a somewhat bulkier stopper knot than the Overhand Knot. The Figure of Eight Knot tied in the bight (fig. 19(L)) forms a stronger loop, and this may be used as a still bulkier stopper knot. The Flemish Bend (fig. 19(M)) is two lines joined by Figures of Eight Knots.

The Phoebe Knot (fig. 19(N)), named after Clifford Ashley's daughter, separates beads on a string. The Double Overhand Knot (fig. 19(P)) can be either a stopper knot or another 'bead knot.

The Crossing Knot (fig. 19(Q)) is used to lock firm crossing points on parcels.

The Running Figure of Eight Knot (fig. 19(R)) is yet another effective packer's noose.

The Crabber's Eye Knot (fig. 19(S)) is a loop knot which may be adjusted for size and then locked by pulling one end.

KNOTS USED IN WEAVING
Weavers work with thinner, weaker threads and yarns. So,

they may use knots not generally recommended for use in rope (because they would jam, say); weavers can cut them off afterwards, or bury them from sight within their creations.

Knots are needed not only on warp (see Glossary) threads and weft wool but also as part of the primitive mechanism which operates the loom. Cords must be anchored to the loom's framework, or passed through holes in it and secured with stopper knots. Treadles must be connected to harnesses or lams. Warp threads must be gathered together and fastened in bundles to apron sticks. Broken threads must be promptly rejoined.

The following knots — some already discussed, others yet to come — will also be useful to weavers and other craftworkers . . . REEF KNOT, OVERHAND KNOT, FIGURE OF EIGHT KNOT, CLOVE HITCH, HIGHWAYMAN'S HITCH, GROUND LINE HITCH and ROUND TURN AND TWO HALF-HITCHES (figs. 12, 9(A), 19(K), 16, 38, 35 and 17 respectively). In addition, there are a few knots peculiar to weaving:

span knot (fig. 20(A))
Tied with a long standing part and a short end, it's used to fasten any cord to the loom, e.g. a third harness at the back; or for connecting treadles to harnesses. The Span Knot is also a way of temporarily fixing a new length of warp thread to a pin in the cloth, so that the two ends of a broken warp thread under tension may be joined.

snitch knot (fig. 20(B))
This is unique to weavers and essential for loom adjustment. It's a non-slip but adjustable knot for attaching heddles to pedals and lams so as to vary the height of the heddle frames. I am assured by weaving friends that it is indispensable; and they add that it is easier to support the weight of certain loom parts during the tying process if the loop comes up from below. To adjust, slide the loop upwards and tighten or loosen the half Reef Knot. Another Snitch Knot may also be improvised (fig. 20(C)) with a single cord; the upper cord tied in a Loop Harness Knot — otherwise a common Packer's Knot (fig. 19(F)), while the ascending lower line

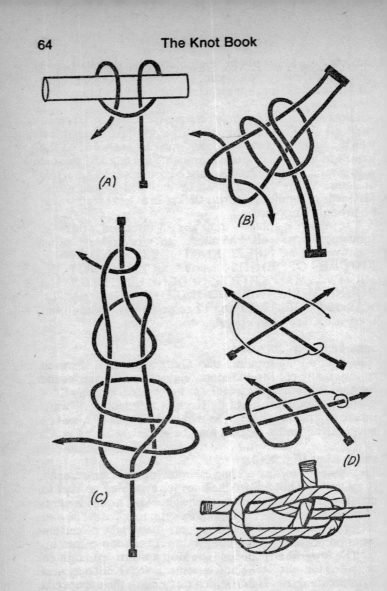

Fig. 20 Weavers' Knots

makes a Sheet Bend with draw loop (fig. 14(E)).

weaver's knot (fig. 20(D))
A great many knots are used to join a new piece of wool (behind the heddle) onto the broken end; but the Sheet Bend (fig. 14), tied a special way, is the common Weaver's Knot. Always hold the end from the warp beam in the non-tying hand to prevent the thread being pulled into the layers of warp beneath it on the beam.

6
MORE GENERAL KNOTS

sheepshank (fig. 21)
In 1627 this was a knot considered vital for all seamen. Strangely, it has become discredited. Some knot books now omit it. I differ. I see uses for it still.

It shortens a rope without cutting it (fig. 21(A)), which saves money. It suspends slack lines out of harm's way (e.g. bellropes). Modified, it is a makeshift purchase, the Waggoner's Hitch (fig. 21(B)) used widely by truck drivers to tighten lorry lashings. N.B. The twist in the long bight is a safeguard which prevents the knot spilling while it is being set up. A Sheepshank will also bridge a weak or damaged portion of a rope (fig. 21(C)) which must nevertheless be used. This is perhaps its most useful — yet least mentioned — function; take care that the suspect portion passes through both half-hitches.

The Sheepshank has many advantages. It is tied in the bight of the rope — needing no ends — and is easily learned. A quick alternative tying method is to make three loops (fig. 21(D)), pulling the centre one out through the other two.

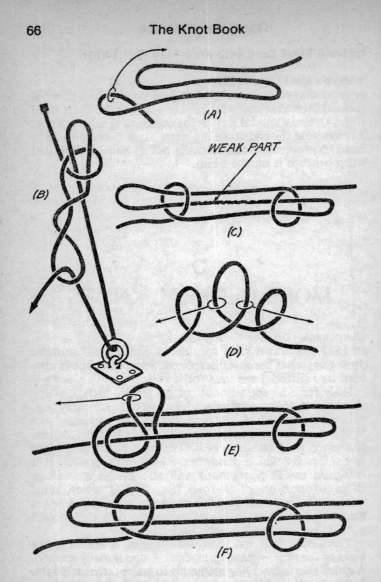

WEAK PART

Fig. 21 Sheepshank

The knot holds under tension but falls apart when slacked off and cannot jam; in fact it is only secure under tension. It may also be tied by forming a loop in the bight (fig. 21(E)) and transferring it with a tug to the single part of the line (fig. 21(F)).

transom knot (fig. 22)
The Transom Knot (fig. 22(A)–(B)) is an excellent way to fix together cross-pieces of wood, bamboo, etc. (such as bean sticks and trellis work in the garden). I fix canoe paddles to my car luggage rack with Transom Knots. It's related to the Constrictor Knot and — like that knot — ends may be cut short for neatness. Also, cut the knot off by severing its diagonal, when it will fall away in two halves; although it can be prised apart with a pricker.

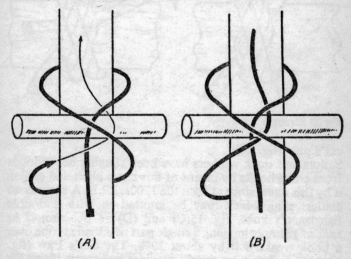

(A)   *(B)*

Fig. 22 Transom Knot

strangle knot (fig. 23)
When used on just a single foundation, the self-same transom knot is a Strangle Knot (fig. 23(A)–(B)); first-rate

for securing the neck of a sack, a roll of wallpaper or inflated balloon. Tuck a draw-loop in a Strangle Knot (fig. 23(C)) and it makes a useful temporary seizing.

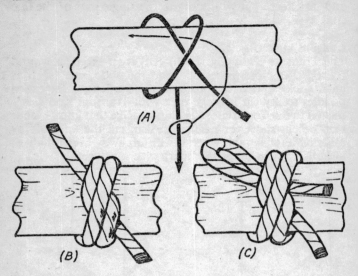

(A)

(B)

(C)

Fig 23 Strangle Knot

cat's paw (fig. 24)
Sailors and dock workers have been slinging heavy loads from crane hooks by means of this strop hitch and calling it by this name since at least the 1700s. (N.B. A strop is an endless sling which may be knotted — with a double fisherman's knot, fig. 15(C) and (D) — but *should be spliced*.) Simply hanging a single part of a loaded rope over a hook weakens it by about 30%. The Cat's Paw (fig. 24(A)–(C)) drawn up snugly provides insurance; if one leg should break, the other may survive long enough to lower the load to the ground.

hangman's (Jack Ketch's) knot (fig. 25)
This is a very strong noose designed to withstand a heavy shock loading! It does not always slide easily and is pre-

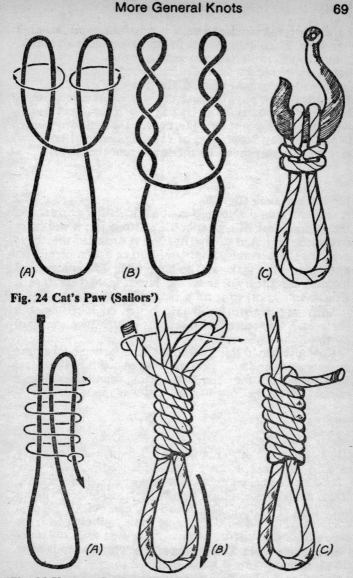

Fig. 24 Cat's Paw (Sailors')

Fig. 25 Hangman's (Jack Ketch's) Knot

adjusted to the required size. I was taught to tie it with 7 turns (fig. 25(A)–(C)). A Chief Petty Officer aboard the old 'Foudroyant' in Portsmouth Harbour once told me it was not permitted to tie Jack Ketch's knot (Jack Ketch was a renowned hangman) aboard Her Majesty's ships of the Royal Navy. A pity, because the way it's tied is a useful lesson. It's the basis for a Heaving Line Knot (fig. 77) and, with a second layer of riding turns atop the first seven turns, is a useful way Scouts had of carrying hanks of cord for emergencies suspended by the loop from their belts.

jug (or jar) sling (fig. 26)

A splendid knot designed to exert a ratchet-like grip around the smooth neck of a glass bottle or stone jar; it will carry containers of liquid safely (fig. 26(F)) provided they have even the slightest raised lip. Useful to campers, picnickers and home wine makers. The large bight forms a natural handle and the two ends are knotted together (use a fisherman's knot) to form a second one.

Soft, stretchy stuff will grip better on hard, smooth surfaces. This secure and ingenious contrivance was used by the Romans.

Cowboys found this knot made an effective hackamore or emergency bridle. The central crossed bights of the actual knot form a bit, the outer loops fitting round the animal's muzzle, while the long handles serve as the reins.

square knot (fig. 27)

(Do not confuse this knot with what the Americans know as a Square Knot, namely the Reef Knot (fig. 12).)

This handsome, symmetrical knot is essentially decorative. It makes an excellent tie for a silk neck scarf worn with an open-necked shirt or blouse, and you can quickly become adept at tying and adjusting it beneath your chin with (or even without) a mirror. It can also be used to secure a tie-belt or waist-cord on a dressing gown, when the ends hang down at just the right angle.

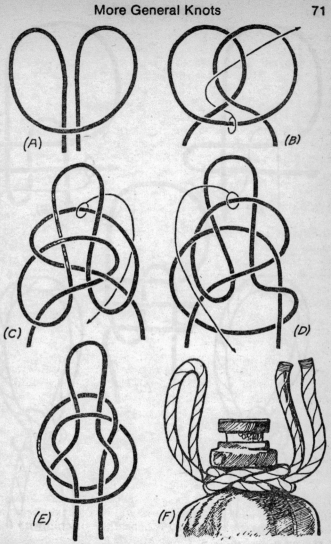

(A) (B)

(C) (D)

(E) (F)

Fig. 26 Jug (or Jar) Sling
(c) Pull rear bight down behind to create layout (D).
(d) Pull front bight down in front to create layout (E)
— completed knot.

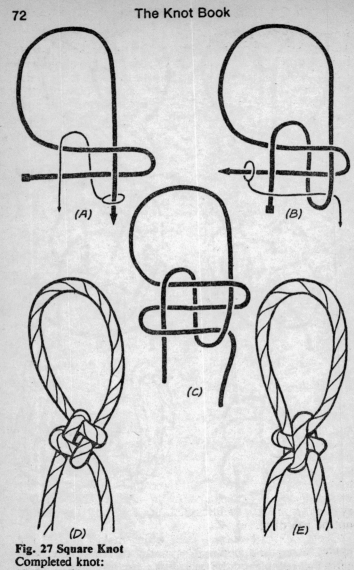

Fig. 27 Square Knot
Completed knot:
(d) Front View
(e) Back View

figure of eight bend (fig. 28)

This is a neat, strong bend (some say it's one of the strongest) in rope as well as short lengths of string. As the Figure of Eight Knot (fig. 19(K)) is still known to many around the world as a 'Flemish Knot', it's also called a 'Flemish Bend'. To tie it in rope, make a Figure of Eight Knot in one end, and then follow it around with the other working end.

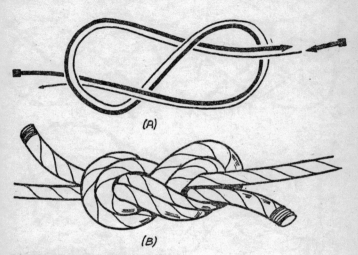

(A)

(B)

Fig. 28 Figure of Eight Bend

full carrick bend (fig. 29)

This is a strong and secure working bend for joining large ropes and cables. The short ends (fig. 29(A)–(B)) should be on opposite sides. Note how it capsizes, when drawn up, into an entirely different configuration (fig. 29(C)). Don't worry. That's what should happen, so let it. The bend will even work in lines of dissimilar size . . . but they should not be too different.

Even soaked it doesn't jam, which makes it ideal for towing lines and anchor cables; and it can be opened with a few light taps from the fat end of a fid (see page 27). I've heard it recommended for climbers, although the ends project at awkward angles and it may prove too bulky to pass through a karabiner. Tied in small cord with both ends on the same side of the knot (fig. 29(D)) it has a distinctive appearance which makes it popular with graphic illustrators and those who embellish bandsmen's uniforms, and is also fine for silk neck scarves and waist-ties.

Fig. 29 Full Carrick Bend

The knot's name may have originated with a Medieval type of Western European ship, the Carrack. Carrick Roads, outside Falmouth, is certainly a location where large numbers of these vessels prepared to sail and trade in convoy. But there could also be an Irish connection. Furthermore, this knot used to be called the Wake Knot and was the heraldic badge of Hereward the Wake, the Saxon leader who refused to yield to William the Conqueror.

surgeon's knot (fig. 30)

Used by surgeons to tie off blood vessels, etc., this knot gets scant attention outside that profession. Yet it's a good knot (fig. 30(A)–(B)). See how it twists (fig. 30(C)) as it is drawn tight, wrapping a diagonal around the top of itself. This must happen if the knot is to be fully secure.

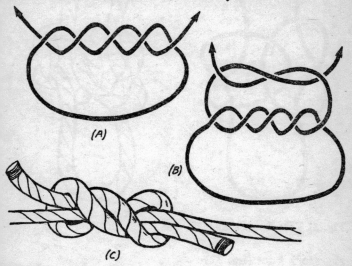

(A)

(B)

(C)

Fig. 30 Surgeon's Knot

true lover's knot (fig. 31)

The basic True Lover's knot (fig. 31(A)–(B)) is of little practical use, except perhaps as a loop knot in very small cord to form a neck lanyard for a whistle or stopwatch, a locket or an amulet of any kind. However see Chapter 9 – Various Other Knots (Rope Ladder, fig. 82). A number of knots, including the Fisherman's Knot (fig. 15), have been called 'True Lover's Knots'. It's a name which seems to have occurred first in 1664, and it's generally agreed to include two Overhand Knots which are interlocked or intertwined to make a pleasing layout. This knot is the start of a very good fancy knot, the Shamrock Knot (fig. 32).

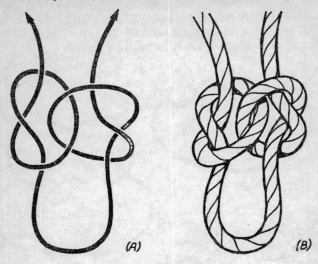

(A)   *(B)*

Fig. 31 True Lover's Knot

shamrock knot (fig. 32)
This attractive, clover leaf knot (fig.32(A)–(B)) has been used by more than one knot book illustrator as an eye-catching cover or title page decoration. It's also nice in ribbon on a gift-wrapped parcel; and can be tied permanently in gold or silver wire to make original jewellery. It looks complicated, but it's only a True Lover's Knot with twin bights pulled out at the sides. Coax it into shape and pull it up tight with care and patience.

rolling (magner's, or magnus) hitch (fig. 33)
The Rolling Hitch (fig. 33(A)–(C)) is obviously related to the Clove Hitch but is designed to take the strain of a lengthwise pull. Sailors, this is a hitch to secure a kicking strap on your dinghy. It is often used to secure a smaller line to a thicker rope, when it should be tied against the lay

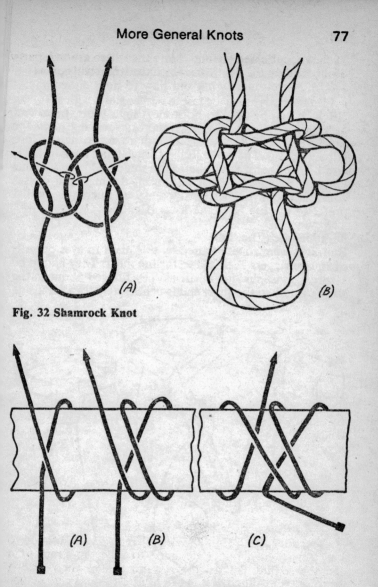

Fig. 32 Shamrock Knot

Fig. 33 Rolling (Magner's, or Magnus) Hitch

of the rope it's tied around. Note that there are two parts of the knot on the side from which the strain will come (fig. 33(C)), so you must work out how to tie it either way.

Flag halyards are made fast to burgee staffs with a Rolling Hitch. It can be used to hoist aloft light tools, pipes and other long objects, or as a temporary mooring hitch for small craft on a tideway, where it is more secure than a Clove Hitch (fig. 16). The name Rolling Hitch dates back to 1841, and before that it could be found under 'M' for Magnus Hitch or Magner's Hitch . . . a label which still causes confusion today. For a really heavy or fluctuating pull I prefer to use the Net Line Knot (fig. 36).

buntline hitch (fig. 34)
Buntlines were ropes secured by this hitch to eyes on sails of square-riggers as an aid to furling them. They had to be secure against shaking adrift as they flogged about in the strong winds so the short end is deliberately trapped inside

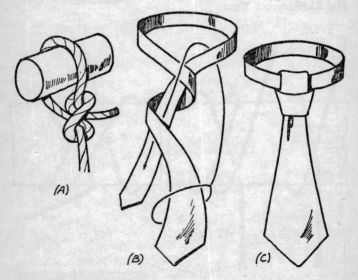

(A)

(B)

(C)

Fig. 34 Buntline Hitch

the Buntline Hitch (fig. 34(A)). This way it tends to jam, but that's its strength and it is the reverse of two natural half-hitches. It's a good packer's knot for parcels, e.g. boned meat, which wants to unfold while you're tying it. Anglers may use it to fasten line to hook or swivel. Don't use it on lifelines or climbing ropes because of its reluctance to come apart, even when it's being untied, due to that short end trapped inside the loop.

Make the Buntline Hitch in flat material (fig. 34(B)–(C)) and you have the knot often found in a man's necktie.

ground line hitch (fig. 35)
This little written about hitch was used extensively at one time by deep sea fishermen to attach drift-nets to the tow-rope, so it's a tough little knot. It was also used to tether cavalry horses to a picket rope. Today's keen young horse and pony riders might like to learn it. Myself, I use it in the end of a coil of line to keep all together.

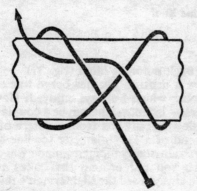

Fig. 35 Ground Line Hitch

net line knot (fig. 36)
Another fisherman's knot, this has the advantage that it has an extra turn around the foundation spar or rope, making it secure against a lengthwise pull in either direction. When I was a frogman working in London's canals and gravel pits,

I learned to fasten my lifeline to my aqualung harness with a short lanyard and the Net Line Knot.

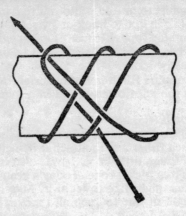

Fig. 36 Net Line Knot

lighterman's back mooring hitch (fig. 37)

Taking in tow a drifting Thames barge was exciting and challenging work which I always enjoyed. Having one of those monsters — laden weight maybe a couple of hundred tonnes — wallowing only feet from the stern of your boat, hung on the end of a 1½″ diameter towline which could part with the strain at any moment, made you choose with care the hitch you put around the oaken towing post 'midships. We always used the Lighterman's Back Mooring Hitch.

First, you take a round turn (or two, if you're unlikely to be able to hold the load otherwise) (fig. 37(A)); then hang on to the line while the coxswain eases the engine ahead and takes up the slack. Once the tow's as you want it, take a bight under and around the taut towrope (fig. 37(B)) and hitch it over the top of the towing post (fig. 37(C)). The working end is finally taken around the post once or twice

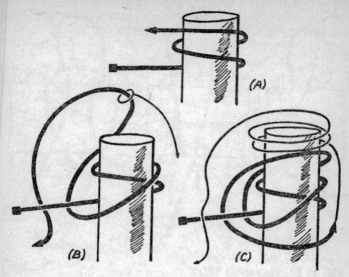

Fig. 37 Lighterman's Back Mooring Hitch

so that it hangs there of its own weight.

This enormously strong hitch will hold anything, yet can be cast free in a few life-saving seconds if things look like going wrong. It is, of course, also first-rate for erecting marquees at fêtes and country shows or for mooring craft when you must make sure the final turns cannot unwrap by attaching the loose hanging end to a convenient cleat.

highwayman's hitch (fig. 38)

The Highwayman's Hitch (fig. 38(A)–(C)) is a slippery hitch, supposedly used by escaping robbers as a rapid release for their horses' reins. It's not featured in nautical manuals. I use it to hold objects temporarily when I need a third hand for craftwork or D.I.Y. (I release it by pulling the end with my teeth); and it would be okay to moor a dinghy during a picnic, leaving a long enough end to be brought back aboard to cast off without stepping ashore again.

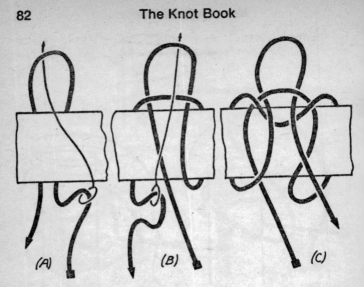

(A)   *(B)*   *(C)*

Fig. 38 Highwayman's Hitch

Horseriders and finders of stray dogs alike can safely tether their animals with this hitch. You might even train your charges to free themselves!

bale sling hitch (fig. 39)
This straightforward way to sling a load from a crane hook with a strop was in great use when sailing ships stocked up

Fig. 39 'Bale Sling Hitch

for months at sea with everything from live pigs to cannon barrels. At the upper end of the strop would be a Cat's Paw (fig. 24).

barrel sling (fig. 40)

How do you sling open containers, still partly full? The answer is the Barrel Sling. A divided Overhand Knot (fig. 40(A)) forms two elbow-like Single Hitches (fig. 40(B)), one

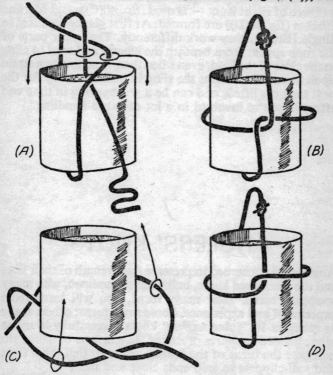

(A)

(B)

(C)

(D)

Fig. 40 Barrel Sling

(a) – (b) Overhand knot forms single hitches which fall away when sling is unhooked.

(c) – (d) Overhand knot laid down like a figure of eight knot forms marline hitches which tend to remain in place when sling is unhooked.

either side of the load. Notice how the upper parts of rope leading to the lifting hook emerge outside the elbow crossings of the Single Hitches. There is no friction to keep them in contact with the load they surround once the weight comes off the sling, and the sling will fall away of its own accord. This is useful if you intend to remove it anyway. When you plan to lift and deposit the load several times using the same sling a slightly different layout — similar to a Figure of Eight Knot — is used (fig. 40(C)), and Marline Hitches (fig. 40(D)) are formed. At first glance identical to Single Hitches, they work differently. The upper parts of the rope appear from beneath the elbows and tend to cling to the sides of the load, even when there is no longer a strain upon them. This retains the sling in position ready for the next time it's lifted, and can be a great saving in time and effort if you're involved in a lot of cargo handling.

7
ANGLERS' KNOTS

Anglers are concerned to preserve the strength of their lines and use specialised knots, bulky but streamlined, with many wrapping turns. How many turns, you will learn from experiment and experience. Some say 5 turns; others make as many as 10. Tying anglers' knots successfully in nylon monofilament requires practised fingers, lots of saliva (to lubricate the turns of the knots), pliers to pull them tight and nail-clippers to snip ends close and neat.

The terms 'bends' and 'hitches' don't feature in anglers' chat. There are just knots . . . my definition of a knot earlier includes anything tied in small stuff. Many traditional angling knots are no longer secure in modern nylon lines. Beginners might prefer to learn their knots in small cordage

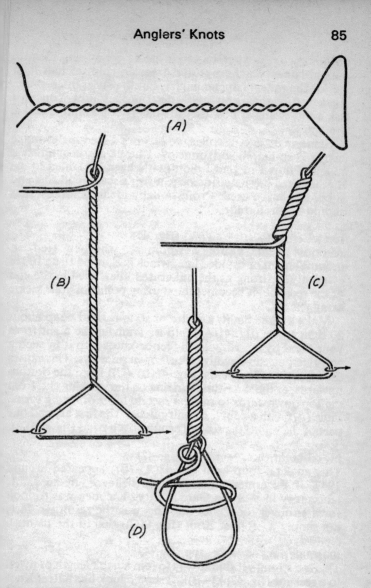

(A)

(B)

(C)

(D)

Fig. 41 Bimini Twist

in home comfort before venturing to cope tying them in monofilament in the wet and freezing cold, at half-light beside the water. I am no angler, but the knots interest me. I can portray them and briefly describe their uses. You must ask another angler how they are incorporated into a tackle system.

Some years ago, a colleague at work asked me to make him a keep-net. Well, somehow I never got around to it . . . and now I'm glad I didn't. It's been explained to me that knotted mesh nets damage a fish's scales and fins and should never be used. Professionally made, knotless, nets should be preferred.

bimini twist (b.s. — 100%) (fig. 41)

A most remarkable newcomer, whether tied in monofilament or braided line, which is claimed to be 100% efficient (as strong as the unknotted line). Tied in the end of the reel line, it becomes the starting point for your tackle arrangement.

Make a large bight, a metre or so long, and wrap about 20 tight twists (fig. 41(A)) into it. Transfer the bight from your hand by inserting both feet or knees into it in such a way that you can steadily force it open sideways. This causes the inset turns to untwist (fig. 41(B)–(C)) from the bottom upwards, at the same time winding on the working end from the top downwards to make a second layer of riding turns. Finish off with a couple of half-hitches, the first around one part of the bight, the second around both parts (fig. 41(D)).

blood bight (b.s. — 80%) (fig. 42)

This anglers' loop knot (fig.42(A)–(B)) appeared around 1947, if fishermen's tales can be believed, at an I.C.I. laboratory in Welwyn Garden City. The idea was to look for a stronger loop knot and this was the result. In fact, it's simply a Stopper Knot (fig. 9(C)) tied in the bight.

loop interlocked with loop (fig. 43)

This is a strong yet simple way to join a hook length of nylon to a reel line (fig. 43(A)–(B)). It should look like a Reef Knot (fig. 12). Don't let it get into a Lark's Head Knot (fig. 43(C)) configuration which is weaker.

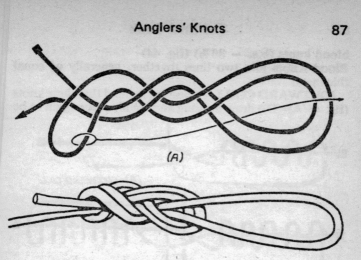

Fig. 42 Blood Bight

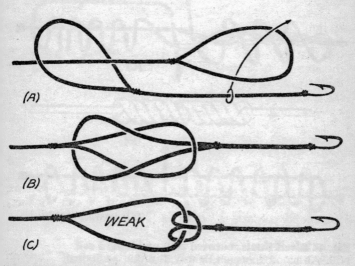

Fig. 43 Loop Interlocked with Loop
(a) – (b) Correct, strong.
(c)   Wrong, weak.

blood knots (b.s. — 80%) (fig. 44)
Blood Knots join two lines together, generally of equal
thickness.

(OUTWARD COIL) . . . Bearing in mind that these knots
(fig. 44(A)–(D)) draw up snug and small, never again to be

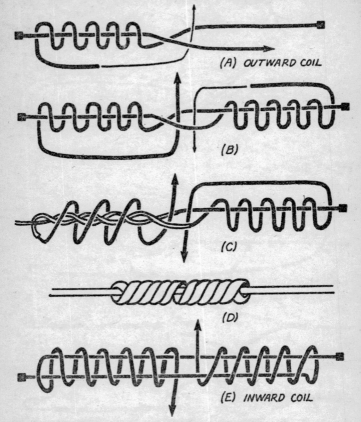

Fig. 44 Blood Knots, outward coil, and inward coil
N.B. All blood knots are tightened so that additional,
contrary-twisting riding turns form as the bight (C) wraps
itself around the existing twists, which unwind a corresponding amount to let it happen.

untied, tackle-makers in the last century were able to keep
how they were tied a trade secret. They'd make you as many
as you wanted, anytime but you had to pay them. Until one
Jock Purvis, an engineer aboard a White Star liner,
ingeniously analysed and reconstructed a specimen knot with
cut sections in paraffin wax plus a microscope. He passed
his discovery to an angling author who told the world in
a 1910 publication. To tighten these knots use the same
technique as for multiple overhand knots (page 41).

(INWARD COIL) . . . This (fig. 44(E)) can be more
difficult to tie but has a neater finish.

improved blood knot (b.s. — 90/100%) (fig. 45)
To join two lines of different sizes, double the thinner line
and wrap it a couple of turns more than the thicker line.

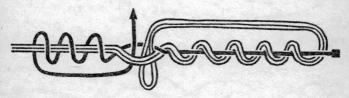

Fig. 45 Improved Blood Knot

perfection loop (fig. 46)
A popular old anglers' loop from about 1870, this knot
survived the change from gut being equally effective in
nylon. It can be tied quickly and easily with practice (fig.
46(A— (B)), but is unsuitable for rope because it jams. A
disadvantage might be the end which protrudes at right-
angles to disturb the water.

water knot (b.s. — 95%) (fig. 47)
The earliest printed reference to this knot (fig. 47(A)) is
believed to be 1496 — just 4 years after Columbus discovered
America — and it was certainly known to Isaak Walton. It
attaches a leader to the reel line, even if the line sizes are
dissimilar. To achieve the great breaking strain claimed for
it, tuck the ends a further 3 times to create a Quadruple

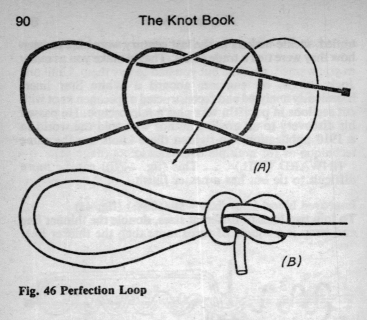

Fig. 46 Perfection Loop

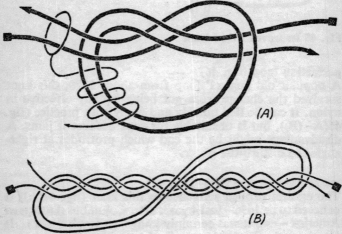

Fig. 47 Water Knot

Overhand Knot (fig. 47(B)) with both lines and draw them up as you would any multiple overhand knot.

loops to line (fig. 48)
A modified Sheet Bend (fig. 48(A)) may be used to attach a fly line to a leader so that the end does not project at right-angles creating unwanted vibrations in the stream. For greatly different sizes of line, use an alternative method (fig. 48(B)).

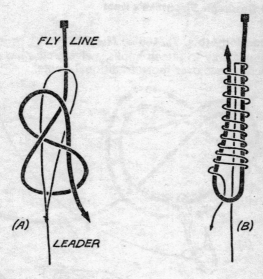

FLY LINE

(A)

LEADER

(B)

Fig. 48 Loops to Line

quadruple fisherman's knot (fig. 49)
This strong, barrel-shaped knot with ends snipped off short, can best be mastered by learning the Fisherman's Knot (fig. 15(A)–(B)) and the Double Fisherman's Knot (fig. 15 (C)–(D)) first.

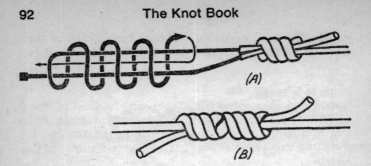

Fig. 49 Quadruple Fisherman's Knot

overhand loop (b.s. 95/100%) (fig. 50)
This simple way to attach hooks, swivels, etc., has gained
wide acceptance over more traditional knots.

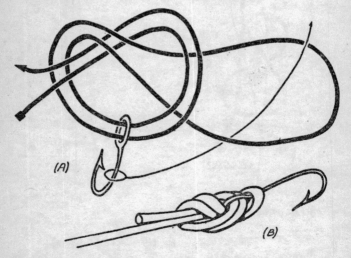

Fig. 50 Overhand Loop

half blood knot (3½ turns) (b.s. – 80%) (fig. 51)
An old, still useful attachment to an eyed hook for thicker

lines, this knot is recommended when the 5 turns of the Improved Tucked Half Blood Knot (fig. 52) will not tighten snugly.

Fig. 51 Half Blood Knot (3½ turns)

improved (tucked) half blood knot (b.s. — 95%) (fig. 52)
Make 5 turns – and double very thin line – to tie this knot.

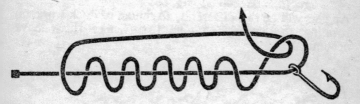

Fig. 52 Improved (tucked) Half Blood Knot

hook tie (b.s. — 95%) (fig. 53)
Another strong attachment to an eye hook.

Fig. 53 Hook Tie

double stevedore knot (fig. 54)

For gut or nylon, it has the advantage of a double thickness around the swivel ring.

Fig. 54 Double Stevedore Knot

cat's paw (b.s. 95/100%) (fig. 55)

Anglers will tie this differently to sailors or dock workers, rotating the swivel, etc. until sufficient turns have accumulated.

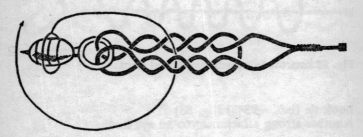

Fig. 55 Cat's Paw (anglers')

turle knot (fig. 56)

Turle knots create a straight pull on any hook with a turned down eye, e.g. fly-tied hooks; and they acquired their name on 30–5–1884 after a Major Turle of Newton Stacey. First pass the line through the hook's eye, then form the knot and bring the hook up through it. The knot is drawn snug on the upper side of the neck of the hook, taking care that the loop passes freely over the hackles of the fly.

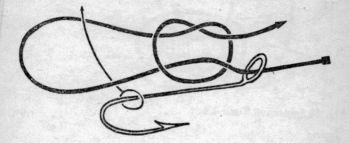

Fig. 56 Turle Knot

double turle knot (fig. 57)
This is a stronger version.

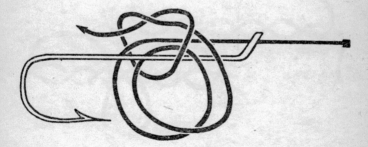

Fig. 57 Double Turle Knot

improved turle knot (b.s. — 75/85%) (fig. 58)
This version of the knot may not be quite as strong as the original Turle Knot but is considered more secure in nylon lines.

Fig. 58 Improved Turle Knot

blood dropper loop (fig. 59)

One of the best and strongest ways to create a paternoster system is to tie a Triple Overhand Knot (fig. 59(A)) and pull down a bight (fig. 59(B)). This obtains the required loop at right angles to the knot.

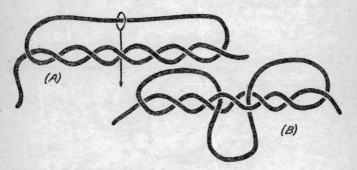

(A)

(B)

Fig. 59 Blood Dropper Loop

whip knot (fig. 60)

This knot exerts a friction grip attaching a leader to a fly line (fig. 60(A)) and should be reinforced by a suitable adhesive. It may be adapted as a secure knot for eyed hooks by reeving the end of the line through the eye first before

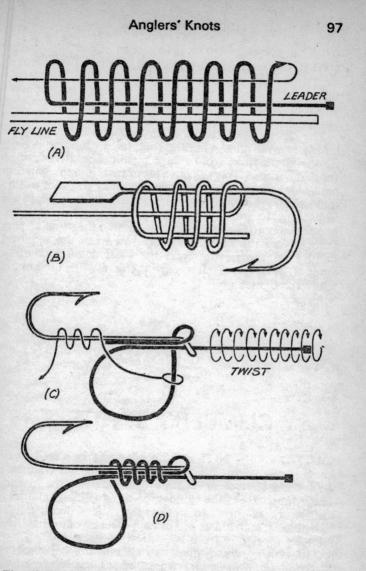

LEADER

FLY LINE

(A)

(B)

(C)

TWIST

(D)

Fig. 60 Whip Knot

tying; but will also work on spade-ended ('blind') hooks (fig. 60(B)). It is most easily made using a short separate length of nylon. The end is passed through the turns before tightening by means of a wire loop, needle (it is sometimes called a 'needle knot') or the hollow tube of a discarded ballpoint pen.

The cleverest way to tie it (fig. 60(C)), once you have clearly in your mind what the completed whipping is like, is to wrap the turns from a large bight deliberately formed for that purpose. This will put a lot of twist into the standing part which must be removed, or tightening the knot will be impossible. When you've seen it happen once or twice, you'll learn how to impart a contrary twist (in this instance anticlockwise) of just the right amount into the standing part before tying the knot. Then, as you wrap the required number of turns, you undo the twist a corresponding amount. When no tension remains (fig. 60(D)), the knot is ready for tightening.

8
CLIMBERS' KNOTS

CAUTION – I'm NOT a climber but simply a student of knots. I can portray and describe them so that beginners may at least learn them in comfort and safety on the ground. They must seek the guidance of qualified climbing instructors in how to make the knots work aloft. Experienced individuals will be able to revise or extend their knotting repertoire from the following selection.

The warning already given (see Chapter 2 – Ropemaking – Synthetic (Manmade) Rope) about manmade ropes melting with friction generated heat, and thus parting without warning, applies especially to nylon climbing ropes. The result could be fatal.

Prusik knot (Dr. Carl Prusik, 1931) (fig. 61)
It's a climbers' device for attaching slings to rope in such a way that they slide when the knot is loose, but seize and

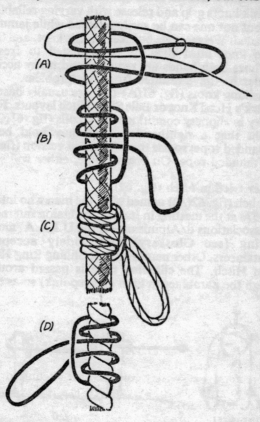

Fig. 61 Prusik Knot
(c) A 6–coil Prusik Knot gives a better grip.
(d) A left-hand Prusik Knot is used on left-handed line.

hold solid under a sideways load. It is used as a safety mechanism when abseiling (or rappelling) (see Glossary) down rock faces; and is also employed with two stirrups for climbing upwards. Rock climbers, cavers, tree surgeons, steeplejacks and others engaged scaling tricky heights all need to know one or more prusik-type knots.

Prusik knots grip and release with varying reliability and ease, but not one can be easily released while jammed and full loaded. Weight must be taken off the knot, and the turns of the knot must then be manipulated to free them; sometimes both hands are required and many accidents — even death — have resulted from this problem.

Prusiking knots (fig. 61(A)–(B)) are usually based upon the Lark's Head Knot or Bale Sling Hitch layouts. For extra security in slippery conditions use 6 coils (fig. 61(C)). It is thought that a righthanded knot may hold better on righthanded rope; so use the lefthanded version (fig. 61(D)) on lefthanded rope. On braided line, either will serve.

Munter friction hitch (fig. 62)
This hitch (fig. 62(A)) named after the man who introduced it in 1974 at the meeting in Italy of the Union Internationale des Associations d/Alpinisme — is the U.I.A.A. method of belaying (see Glossary) and widely accepted by mountaineers. Other names include Sliding Ring Hitch and Italian Hitch. The climbing rope is passed around and through the karabiner (a kind of snap-link) so as to arrest

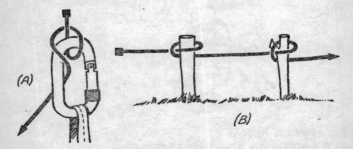

(A)

(B)

Fig. 62 Munter Friction Hitch

a falling climber by locking up; and it can also be paid out
or pulled in to give slack or tension as required. It can be
used for abseiling but the practice is hard on the rope. (This
dynamic hitch is based on the static Crossing Knot (fig.
62(B)) still used today to stake out paths and erect barrier
ropes at fairs and roadworks.

double Munter friction hitch (fig. 63)
The single version (fig. 62) works fine with standard 11mm.
rope, but smaller diameter rope such as 9mm., often needs

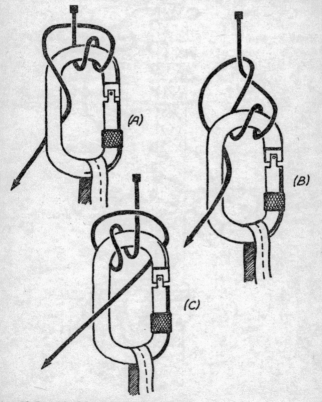

Fig. 63 Double Munter Friction Hitch

more friction and this heavy duty version (fig. 63(A)) provides it. The hitch may be tied in reverse (fig. 63(B)–(C)).

penberthy knot (Caver's Helical Knot) (fig. 64)
This knot and its variants are more reliable than the Prusik Knot and cannot truly jam; but are not easily released when loaded. Cavers reportedly find it effective.

There are 3 basic versions (fig. 64(A)–(C)) with closures which have been described as either Sheet Bends or distorted

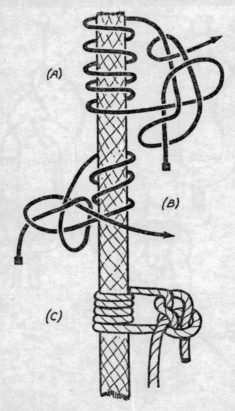

Fig. 64 Penberthy Knot

Bowlines. It is a very open knot and both the number of turns (from 4 to 9) and the amount of slack must be adjusted – with experience – to the weight of the person, the rope diameters involved and the material used. Too much slack and it slips; too little and it's hard to move. Opinions are divided whether the turns should be wound upwards or downwards but, if laid rope is used, there is an advantage from winding WITH the lay.

hedden knot (cross prusik knot) (fig. 65(A))

Held to be about as good as the Prusik, it's harder to loosen but the Double Hedden Knot (fig. 65(B)) gives more friction. It has a slightly different appearance, even when tied identically (fig. 65(C)–(E)), in slings of different sizes or with a twist. If tied upside down (fig. 65(F)) it will slip, as the knot is directional in its ability to hold.

tarbuck knot (fig. 66)

The Tarbuck Knot became obsolete with the advent of Kernmantel (sheath-and-core) double braid ropes. These new lines absorb shock elastically and the sheath of a Kernmantel rope would be stripped by the slide-and-grip action of the Tarbuck Knot. So new knots have been developed and the Tarbuck Knot is rarely mentioned in modern climbing texts. The Figure of Eight Loop (fig. 70) is now used more than any other as the standard tie-in directly to the harness. The Tarbuck Knot (fig. 66(A)–(B)) will remain a useful addition to the collection of general purpose knots. It's an adjustable loop. The actual knot can be grasped in the hand and slid along the rope but it grips and holds under strain; so it remains suited for improvised tent guys, mooring small craft in a tideway, etc., when lives do not depend directly upon it.

alpine butterfly knot (fig. 67)

A picturesque name for what is thought by many to be the best non-slip loop tied in the bight. It is a middle-man's knot for climbers which fits around the chest and can be hauled on from either direction. Note the crossing point where the bight emerges from the neck of the two interlocked loops (fig. 67(B)). This is the hallmark of a properly made Alpine Butterfly Knot.

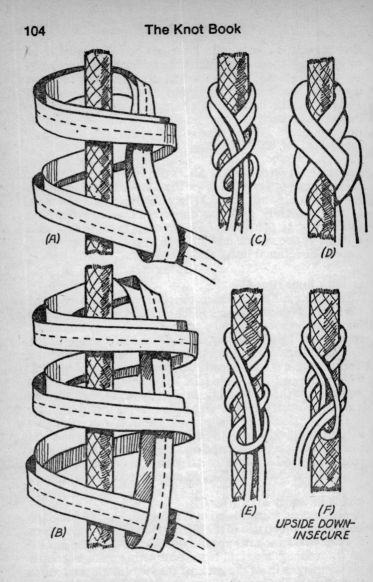

(A)

(B)

(C)

(D)

(E)

(F)
UPSIDE DOWN-
INSECURE

Fig. 65 Hedden Knot

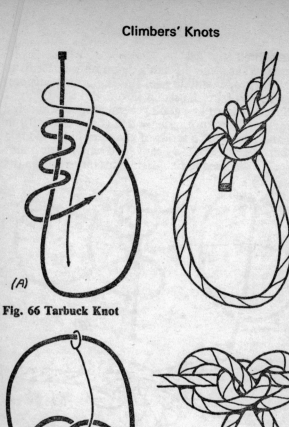

(A)

Fig. 66 Tarbuck Knot

(B)

(A)

Fig. 67 Alpine Butterfly Knot

(B)

manharness hitch (fig. 68)

It has been used as a middleman's tie-on but – it seems to me – lacks the proper stability for this important purpose, being designed to take the strain in one direction only. I suggest it's learned just as a good general purpose knot. It's a very practical loop knot quickly tied (fig. 68(A)–(B)) in the bight and can make a series of shoulder loops along a rope so that men may pull a heavy load while their hands remain free. It was used to haul field guns into position (its

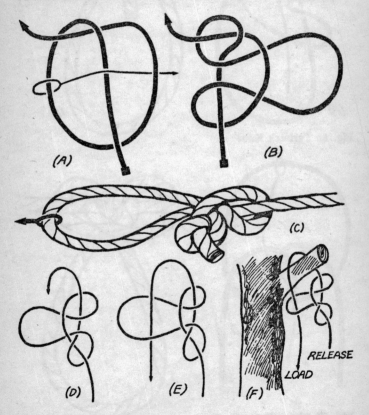

(A)

(B)

(C)

(D)

(E)

(F)

RELEASE

LOAD

Fig. 68 Manharness Hitch

other name being Artilleryman's Hitch); or to help horses
(Harness Loop) when the going under hoof was heavy.
Authorities agree it's a one-way hitch but nobody illustrates
which way. I've always assumed it to be as shown (fig.
68(C)). It's possible to middle a climbing rope, using a
Manharness Hitch, to descend one part of the rope and then
recover it by pulling on the other part (fig. 68(D)–(F)).

frost knot (fig. 69)

The Frost knot is just a simple overhand or thumb knot tied
in webbing.

A series of Frost Knots can be used (fig. 69(B)) in the tying

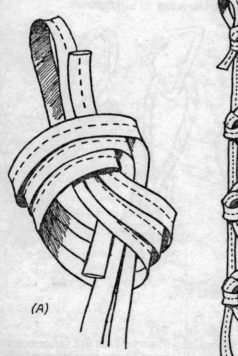

(A)   (B)

Fig. 69 Frost Knot

of webbing stirrups called 'etriers', which take the form of
a sort of improvised rope ladder.

figure of eight loop (fig. 70)

A widely used fixed loop, this has many applications. It
attaches a line to a karabiner (fig. 70(A)–(B)). Or, using a
bight as a working end pulled through the climber's
waistband, the active rope may be anchored with an
adaptation called an Anchor Knot (fig. 70(C)). Its advantage
over Alpine Butterfly Knots and others is simplicity. It is
unmistakeable and therefore quickly checked by a team
leader. But see Chapter 10 – New Knots – for two
variations. Three Quarter Figure of Eight Loops (fig. 94)
are worthy of consideration as alternatives.

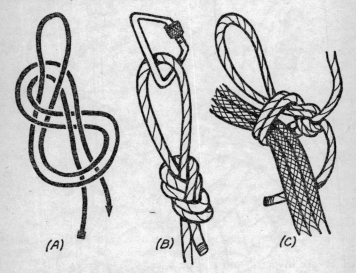

(A)   (B)   (C)

Fig. 70 Figure of Eight Loop

bowline in the bight (fig. 71)

A reliable knot with a long history of sea use for rescue work
or to sling an object, this knot forms two loops which do

not slide. The secret of the Bowline in the Bight is that, although most parts of the knot are made in the doubled rope (fig. 71(A)—(B)), the bight around the standing parts is itself only single (fig. 71(C)); and this single bight must be passed over the entire knot to complete the tying process.

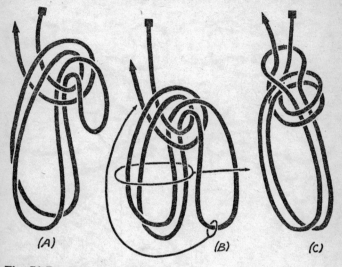

(A)   (B)   (C)

Fig. 71 Bowline in the Bight

fireman's chair knot (fig. 72)

This versatile rescue knot has been taught to Fire Brigades, Coastguards, mountain rescue teams, first aiders and many others engaged in emergency services. It's for lifting and lowering from heights persons unconscious, disabled or otherwise in peril; and can be speedily tied in the bight.

Tie a Handcuff Knot (fig. 72(A)—(C)). Do NOT use a Tom Fool's Knot (it occurs if the loops (B) are not interlaced correctly (fig. 72(D))) which is weaker. Slip one loop over the patient's head, around their back and under their armpits. The other loop goes around both legs behind the knees. Adjust them to size and lock each loop in place (fig.

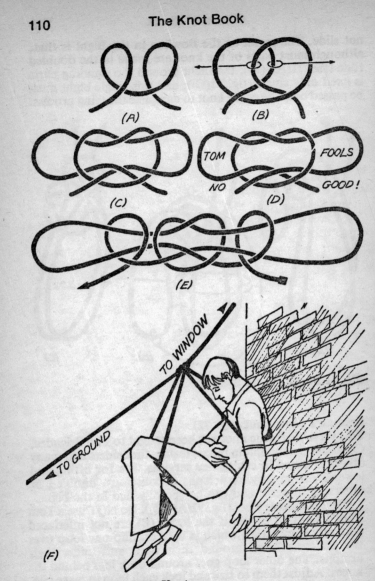

Fig. 72 Fireman's Chair Knot

72(E)) with a half-hitch. The standing end of the rope is then used to raise or lower the load, while the working end is pulled by a second person to hold the patient away from bumping against vertical walls, cliff faces, etc., (fig. 72(F)). Most of these so-called 'Handcuff Knots' started life, I suspect, for the more mundane purposes of hobbling animals overnight to limit them straying. WARNING: Unconscious patients are heavy, floppily unmanageable, and liable to fall out of any fixed loop knot to further serious injury or even death; unless you make sure each bight is tightened to grip the individual.

triple bowline (fig. 73)
Tie a Bowline with a bight of line, i.e. make it with a doubled rope throughout (fig. 73(A)) (NOT a true Bowline in the Bight). Draw the end of the bight downwards through the knot (fig. 73(B)) to form a third loop. A useful variation, this is recommended for rescue and salvage purposes.

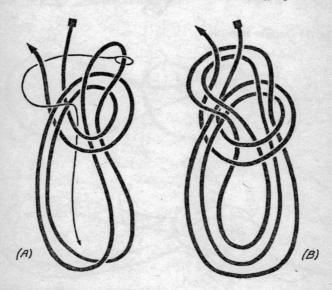

(A)   (B)

Fig. 73 Triple Bowline

ontario bowline (fig. 74) and algonquin bowline (fig. 75)
The Bowline (fig. 13) and the Figure of Eight Loop (fig. 70) tend to spill or drift, sometimes coming undone, if they

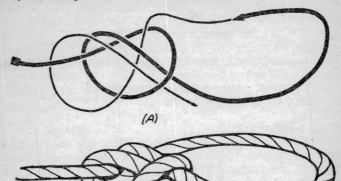

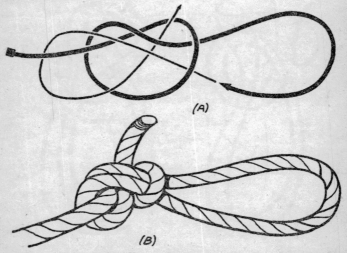

(A)

(B)

Fig. 74 Ontario Bowline

(A)

(B)

Fig. 75 Algonquin Bowline

cannot be fully tightened. These two loops (figs. 74–75) seem to overcome that weakness in older, stiffer climbing ropes.

one way sheet bend (fig. 76)

The common Sheet Bend (fig. 14) suffers from the disadvantage that one end sticks out more or less at right-angles with an increased chance that the knot may jam in a rocky crevice. Modifying the Sheet Bend (fig. 76) so that

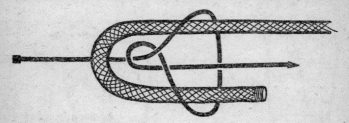

Fig. 76 One Way Sheet Bend

both ends lie back away from the direction in which the rope is to be hauled is something climbers especially should consider. It could be a useful trick for hauling electric cables through cavity walls and beneath floorboards when rewiring the house.

9
VARIOUS OTHER KNOTS

heaving line knot (fig. 77)

A heaving line is a light line which acts as a 'messenger' (i.e. it's sent on ahead) for a heavier line when it is thrown to a pier, or another vessel. The heavier line is then pulled across the gap. The end of the heaving line must be weighted to aid in throwing. A climber may just add a snaplink to lob his line clear of a rocky ridge or crest. But, in boating circles, there's often someone waiting to catch the line . . . so the end must be soft. The Heaving Line Knot can, with practice, be improvised in seconds (fig. 77(A)–(D)) and won't hurt anyone.

Heaving lines will be about 10–15mm. diameter and up

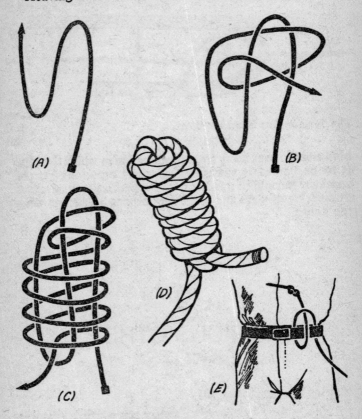

Fig. 77 Heaving Line Knot

to 25 metres long. A flexible, braided texture is ideal. Boat heaving lines should float and be strong enough to tow a man through water.

You must keep your end of a heaving line secure. It's not usual to bend it onto the heavier rope or cable before it's been thrown successfully. So, you may stand on the end or loop it round your wrist. An effective trick is to tuck a bight up inside your belt or climbing harness, pass the end through with a Figure of Eight Knot tied in it as a stopper, and draw the resulting Crossing Knot (fig. 77(E)) snug. Do not however fasten yourself to a heaving line if there is a risk that you will be hauled overboard, e.g. by your craft overshooting its mooring or berth after the thrown end has been caught and secured.

heaving line bend (fig. 78)
It remains to bend your light messenger line to the heavy rope that will follow it. Sheet Bends and Double Sheet Bends (fig. 14) are often impractical because the sizes of the lines are too dissimilar (the thicker bight would straighten itself out, spilling the bend apart). A 'racking' bend (fig. 78), so called because of its figure-of-eight (or 'racking') seizing turns which draw the sides of the thick bight together, is the solution.

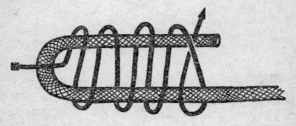

Fig. 78 Heaving Line Bend

parbuckle (fig. 79)
Recently I took delivery of an enormous piece of joinery weighing possibly one hundred kilos. It was a flight of

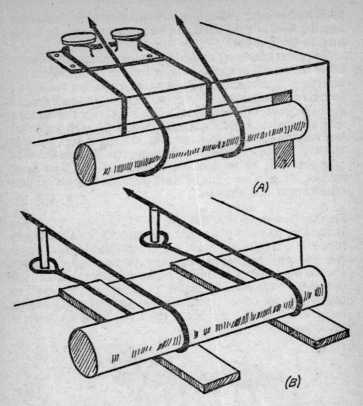

(A)

(B)

Fig. 79 Parbuckle

wooden steps, complete with handrails, purpose built for
my steeply terraced back garden. The assembly was too big
to go through any door. So, single-handed, using a ladder
as an inclined ramp and a 2″ hawser, I rolled it up and over
my garage roof and lowered it triumphantly into the back
yard. Mind you, before I got the hang of it, I nearly dropped
it on the roof of my new car! The improvisation which did
the trick was a Parbuckle.

It needs little explanation, working best with round objects
(casks, kegs, canisters, logs, etc.) since there's very little

friction as they roll with the movement of the rope. So almost all your effort is converted into work. One person can do the work of two. A doubled line (fig. 79(A)) is sufficient for short lengths of load. Longer loads need two separate lines (fig. 79(B)). Guide and control the load with care, applying equal strain to each line or it may cant and slip out of control.

MAKESHIFT PURCHASE (fig. 80)
With this purchase, even the weak can raise heavy loads.

Fig. 80 Makeshift Purchase

Allowing for friction it still nearly doubles their pulling power. Don't stand beneath the load. Use a tough sling or strop; that's where the wear occurs. Reinforce the tree limb or other overhead support with sacking to minimise damage. To lift the load 1 metre you will need to pull down 2 metres of line.

FIRST AID

Bandages and slings should be tied off with Reef Knots (fig. 12); or, better still, a Reef Bow which can be undone easily with the least discomfort to the patient. Tie knots on the uninjured side but be prepared to vary that rule to avoid patients having to lie upon knots. The Greeks and Romans used the Reef Knot to fix medical dressings 2,000 B.C. They believed wounds healed quicker if this knot was used. It appears we're keeping the tradition but have forgotten the reason.

PARCEL TYING (fig. 81)

All shopkeepers used to be expert at tying parcels with string in the days before adhesive tape and pre-packaged foods. Each purchase needed to be separately and speedily parcelled up for every customer. Children would watch amazed as the butcher or grocer, fingers moving faster than the eye could properly follow, formed and tightened knots without a pause in his sales patter. The whole process was done automatically by them — quicker than thought — appearing like some sort of conjuring trick.

Here is how they did it or, at least, one way. It works best with thin twine. I hear it's still sometimes used in the Post Office to repair damaged parcels, so it's a method worth learning.

(a) Pass the working end from your ball of twine under the parcel, back across the top, and then lead it around its standing part. Form a noose (fig. 81(A)), leaving a generous tail-end which will be used to tie-off later;

(b) Lever the standing part backwards and forwards to tighten both the slip knot you've just tied and the grip of the twine around the parcel, until it holds firmly without any further help from you (fig. 81(B));

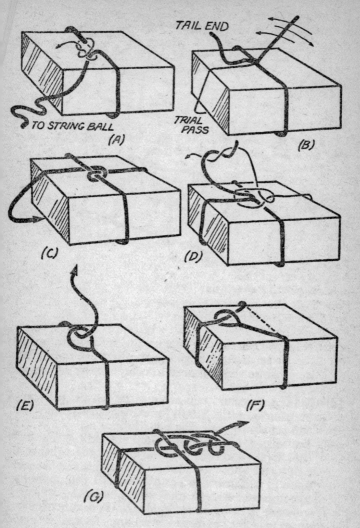

Fig. 81 Parcel Tying

The Knot Book

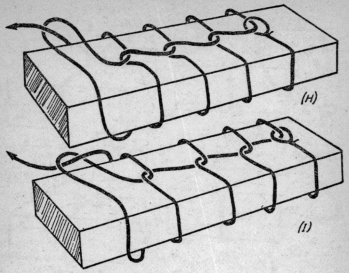

Fig. 81 (cont.) Parcel Tying
(h) Single Hitches
(i) Marline Hitches

(c) Now you can make a trial pass with the twine around the parcel at right angles to the first bit, decide how much more you will need to complete the parcel, and cut it with some to spare;

(d) Make the second trip around the parcel, forming a crossing knot (fig. 81(C)) for extra security at the back, and return to your original slip knot;

(e) To finish off, take a half hitch around the first knot (fig. 81(D)) and then use both ends of the string to tie half a reef knot atop the lot. Thin twine can be relied upon to bed down and grip nicely but you might like to complete the reef knot for your own peace of mind.

If you have to tie up crates, cabin trunks or other jumbo-sized loads, use thick cordage — even rope if necessary — and adopt the following more robust method of doing the job.

Use a Running Bowline (fig. 13(D)) or an Overhand Loop

(fig. 10(C)) or some other Packer's Knot (fig. 19(E)–(G)) to make a loop and pass this around your parcel (fig. 81(E)). Lead the working end at right-angles around one end of the parcel, exerting sufficient tensions to pull the original turn around the parcel into a slight 'V' shape (fig. 81(F)). On the reverse side of the package (fig. 81(C)) form a Crossing Knot (fig. 19(Q)); and return to the start once more. Pull the 'V' shape out straight with the final tuck of the string, which will tighten everything up nicely, and finish with a couple of half-hitches (fig. 81(G)).

Long parcels (fig. 81(H)–(I)) are enclosed with as many hitches as necessary, and a corresponding number of Crossing Knots (fig. 19(Q)) on the reverse side. Use single or Marline Hitches (see fig. 40 for the difference).

ROPE LADDER (fig. 82)

A Frenchman first published this neatly knotted rope ladder (fig. 82(A)–(C)) at the beginning of the century as a boat's ladder for bathers. Each rung is wide enough to insert just

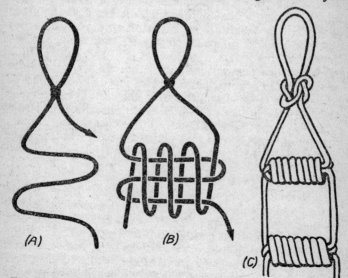

(A)   *(B)*   *(C)*

Fig. 82 Rope Ladder

one foot. Even then it uses a lot of line, so it's only suited for a short ladder but it's still a handy idea to know. The upper bight is formed by a True Lover's Knot (fig. 31).

CLIMBING ROPE
To improvise a climbing rope which almost anyone could use in an emergency, tie a series of Alpine Butterfly Knots at conveniently spaced intervals. (See page 105).

CAR TOW ROPES
The thicker your tow rope is, the better. Sudden snatches can snap even the strongest ropes, especially if led around sharp edges such as the inside of a bumper bar or a towing eye. Use nylon, which stretches. Protect it with sacking where it is likely to chafe. (N.B. It's easier to bandage the rope with rags than to try to pad the bumper of the car).

To secure a tow rope, double a long bight which should be passed underneath the front of the vehicle and around the manufacturer's recommended anchor point on your vehicle. Pull out the bight until it is clear of the front bumper, spot-lights, registration plate and other obstructions. Tie Julie's Hitch (fig. 93) and secure the end to the standing part with a Bowline (fig. 13). Julie's Hitch needs just one pass around the anchorage point, provides two loops as anchorage and enables all the knotting to be done with a clear view away from the car. The two turns which are the heart of the hitch absorb much of the strain of towing; one bight pulling into the other during sudden changes of direction can soak up further undesirable stresses within the hitch.

VEHICLE RECOVERY (fig. 83)
Bogged down? Snowed in? Wheels spinning? It's a helpless feeling and simply pressing down on the accelerator and revving the engine only makes it worse. Selecting 2nd gear and a few rev's — just enough to turn the car's road wheels without stalling — is the right way. Even then, you often need a helpful push or pull applied at the same time. Solid ground and a grip for the tyres may be only a metre or two away.

The Waggoner's Hitch (fig. 21(B)), that modification of

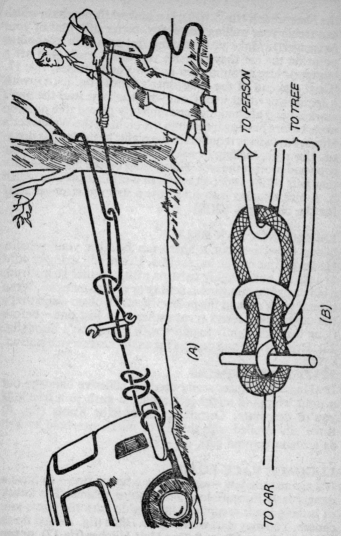

Fig. 83 Vehicle Recovery

the Sheepshank (fig. 21(F)), is a makeshift purchase which can treble your pulling power (or, better still, that of your passenger!). Make your towline fast to a firm anchorage point on the car (have a care, you could easily pull off a bumper). Use a round turn and two half hitches, fig. 17. 'Dog' one end of the Waggoner's Hitch (fig. 83(A)) with a spanner or other item from your toolbox; lead the line's working end around that conveniently placed tree or lamp post, before passing it through the bight of the Waggoner's Hitch. No twist is required in the bight, as the loop is dogged. Use rags, sacking or thick polythene sheets to pad the rope and protect the tree. Harsh wear on the bight can ruin that part of the rope; although in a crisis it may be worth it. A nice solution is to substitute a strop of stronger stuff for the bight (fig. 83(B)).

EMERGENCY FAN BELT
Never travel without a spare fan belt for your vehicle. However, one can be improvised. Use strong string or cord or tear up and roughly twist or plait together strips from a lady's tights, thin garden netting or similar material. Wrap several turns around the pulley wheels involved – and that's the only trick, several turns rather than just one – before tying the ends tightly together with a Surgeon's Knot (fig. 30). Drive gently and only as far as the next service station.

SPLIT HOSE REPAIRS
Leaking water hoses really need an adhesive bandage but a tight whipping might just reduce a gush to a trickle if you're desperate. Certainly, Constrictor Knots (fig. 6) forcefully applied with the aid of pliers, can hold as well as a manufactured clip.

LUGGAGE RACK LOADS
It's against the law – and there's a heavy fine – to have a dangerously insecure load on a motor vehicle. The knack of lashing loads securely is little to do with the knots you choose. You may start with a Clove Hitch (fig. 16) and finish off with a Round Turn & Two Half-Hitches (fig.17), or use entirely different knots. What is crucial is that you have the

imagination to foresee what could happen to your load during the journey should you be forced to brake, accelerate or corner harshly. Obviously, it could shoot off the front, slide backwards, or roll off sideways. So, you must tie it on so that none of those things can occur.

A small box may only need a couple of lashings across from side to side and another couple from front to back. Use separate short lengths. They're easier to tie and, if ever one did work loose, the others are unaffected. Use flat tape or braid which has more grip and will not score grooves into expensive suitcases or antique furniture, and swig each one tight (see 'Swigging', fig. 11). An oar or canoe paddle or a length of copper piping for that D.I.Y. plumbing job will be secure with a couple of Transom Knots (fig. 22): whereas a rolled up carpet will need two separate lashings of some sort a long way apart.

Having made the load inseparable from the luggage rack, you have a new problem. The load may now pull the rack off the car. You may have to tie it onto the vehicle. Older ones had projecting door handles which could be used as belaying points for your lashings. Modern cars have nothing suitable, unless you wind down the windows and pass a line right through the interior of the car.

water knot (fig. 84)
Hundreds of thousands of young swimmers train in clubs and just as many bathe for fun. Most of them now wear anti-chlorine goggles and, when the rubber head strap breaks, it's difficult to tie the stretchy wet rubber bands together again. The best knot I've found to do it is – appropriately – the Water Knot. It grips securely; it's easy to tie and it doesn't use too much of the remaining strap.

Simply make an Overhand Knot (fig. 84(A)) in one of the broken ends. Then insert the other end (fig. 84(B)) and follow the knot around. Work the knot snug and tight (fig. 84(C)) before putting the goggles back on.

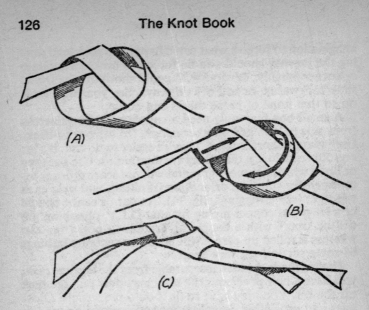

Fig. 84 Swimmers' Goggles Repair (water knot)

10
NEW KNOTS

"Maybe the infant Raleigh, playing wistfully with string,
Took one more turn by accident, and stumbled on the
thing."

(A. P. Herbert)

Inventing a new knot has been likened to an astronomer
spotting a new comet . . . it happens, but not often. Anyone

can take a piece of line, make a few random tucks and come up with something which isn't in the knot books, calling it a new knot. To be any good and worth adopting it should also be (A) of some use, (B) as simple as possible (C) readily learnt and tied, (D) easily untied, (E) both strong and secure, and (F) it should have a distinctive, readily recognized form. The knots which follow are all those things and — I believe — are also relative newcomers on the knotting scene.

rigger's (Hunter's) bend (fig. 85)

On Friday, 6th October 1978, the Times newspaper carried a front page column 11″ long reporting that retired consultant physician Dr. Edward Hunter had invented a new knot. In fact, he'd devised it some years earlier but was only now being made aware that it didn't feature in the knotting literature. The media grabbed the story with enthusiasm. Dr. Hunter was interviewed on radio and T.V. Knot-tying fans wrote in from Europe and America for more information.

Hunter's Bend (fig. 85(A)) — as the Press labelled it — is a strong, simple bend based upon two interlocked Overhand Knots. The Royal Aircraft Establishment (Materials Dept.) tested it to breaking point in parachute cordage and found it ". . . not as strong as the blood knot (fig. 44), similar to the reverse Figure of Eight (fig. 28) and stronger than the Fisherman's Bend (presumably, fig. 15), Sheet Bend (fig. 14) or Reef Knot (fig. 12)".

It's simply tied. Holding both strands together and parallel, throw a loop (with no accidental crossovers but keeping both strands parallel), then tuck each working end through the loop from opposite sides (fig. 85(B)) and coax the knot into its final form (fig. 85(C) — front view; fig 85(D) — rear view). It can even be tied as a loop knot (fig. 85(E)).

Then, with publicity at its height, it was learned that Hunter's Bend is not new. An American, Phil. D. Smith (now sadly deceased) had worked it out for himself in 1943 while he was employed on the San Francisco waterfront during World War II; and he had actually published it in his booklet 'Knots for Mountaineers' in the U.S.A. in the 1950s, calling it simply a Rigger's Bend.

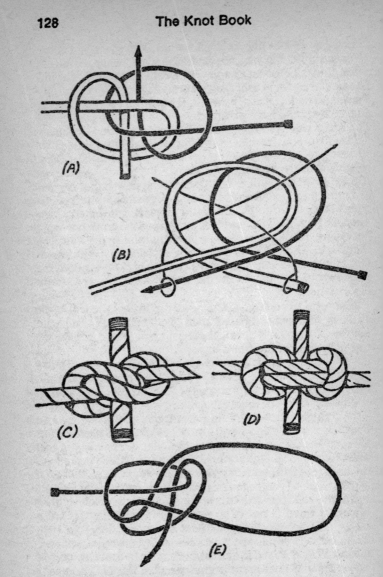

Fig. 85 Rigger's (Hunter's) Bend

tumbling thief knot (centre-tucked) (fig. 86)
Desmond Mandeville of South London is a prolific knot
inventor. He has so many new knots to his credit that he
has worked his way through the alphabet from 'A' to 'Z'
giving them delightful names . . . like Poor Man's Pride and
Tumbling Thief.

The common Thief Knot (fig. 86(A)) resembles a Reef
Knot, but distorts and slips in a totally unreliable way
because its short ends are on opposite sides. Mr. Mandeville
found that by loosening the knot and then crossing the ends
over (fig. 86(B)–(C)) it could be persuaded to jam every time.
Breaking it open by tugging one end away from the standing
part of the rope in the same manner as capsizing a Reef Knot
into a Lark's Head Knot (fig. 12(E)–(F)) caused a double
tripping action (hence, the Tumbling Thief Knot). Not
satisfied with a knot which only worked when nursed
carefully into shape, he further tucked each end in turn right
through the centre of the knot (fig. 86(D)). The resulting
new bend (fig. 86(E)) is secure, strong and good looking.
The unreliable thief has become respectable and taken up
useful work as a bend to join large hawsers.

poor mans' pride (fig. 87)
Knotting goes back so far in time it isn't surprising there's
not much new to be discovered but a lot also gets forgotten.
Dr. Hunter shone a spotlight on Phil Smith's Rigger's Bend
which it hadn't had before (page 127). Desmond Mandeville
found this knot (fig. 87(A)) for himself in 1961, and sent
it to me for scrutiny during all the excitement over Hunter's
Bend. It took about a year to uncover the truth. It's really
the Rosendahl Bend (otherwise known as the Zeppelin
Knot), named after Charles Rosendahl, commander of the
U.S. rigid airship Los Angeles, who apparently insisted his
craft be moored with this bend. That was back in the 1930s
when it was claimed to be superior to the Carrick Bend (fig.
29), Bowline (fig. 13) or Sheet Bend (fig. 14), and that it
could always be untied quickly. A snag with Commander
Rosendahl's favourite bend seemed to be that we couldn't
tie it as slickly as Hunter's Bend; until Ettrick Thomson of
Suffolk came up with a very neat solution (fig. 87(B)–(D)).

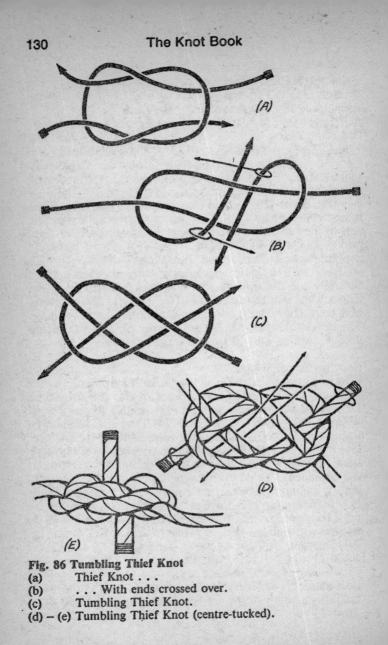

Fig. 86 Tumbling Thief Knot
(a)   Thief Knot . . .
(b)   . . . With ends crossed over.
(c)   Tumbling Thief Knot.
(d) – (e) Tumbling Thief Knot (centre-tucked).

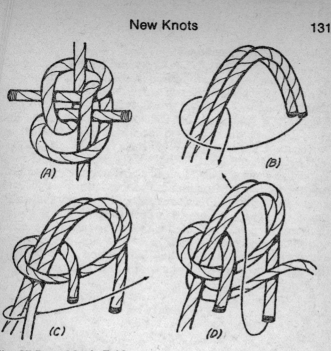

Fig. 87 Poor Man's Pride

bend 'x' (fig. 88)
This is another of Desmond Mandeville's ideas; it is a rope
shortening, readily adjustable, or a tensioning device, which
(unlike the Sheepshank) cannot fall apart but it needs
working ends which the Sheepshank, being tied in the bight,
does not.

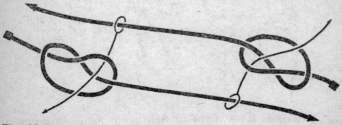

Fig. 88 Bend 'X'

release hitches (figs. 89-90)

Canadian Bob Chisnall is an experienced mountaineer with a mighty sensible concern to find the best knots for climbing. These two Release Hitches were devised by him to overcome the shortcomings of other prusik-type knots (e.g. figs. 61, 64, 65). It is suggested that Release Hitches properly used should reduce the chances of accidents considerably.

Release Hitches (figs. 89-90) have two ends, a load end and a release end (figs. 89(B)-90(B)). The load end of the knot runs from the usual set of turns wrapped around the rappel line, and any loading of this end naturally causes the knot to grip the line. The release end runs parallel to the rappel line, and is contained by each wrap of the knot. Once jammed, the knot is released with a sharp tug on the release end. The uppermost wrap is caused to slip, and it in turn causes the one below it to slide. This action is spread down through the series of coils or wraps until each one is freed and the knot slides.

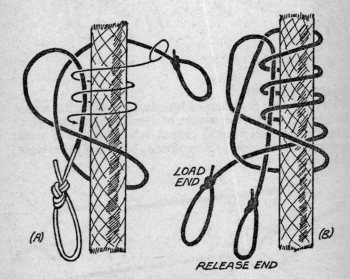

Fig. 89 Release Hitch (Bottom Load)

The two Release Hitches (figs. 89–90) depicted have advantages and disadvantages. The Release Hitch (bottom load version) (fig. 89(A)–(B)) is more secure than the Prusik Knot, will grip even when sloppily tied but tends to drift apart when loaded if there is any slack. The release end then has to be tugged very hard to cause slippage. When tied neatly, bottom load release hitches like this one can be freed easily. Release Hitches (top loaded) (fig. 90(A)–(B)) are just the opposite. If the knot is the least bit sloppy or loose it will slide before jamming, or it may even fail. If it is not snug it will slide several feet as it is tightened before coming to rest. However, it releases readily.

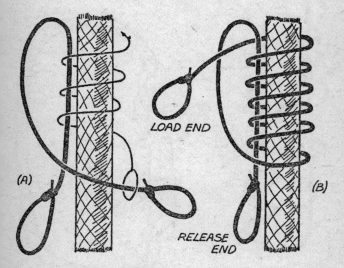

LOAD END

(A)

(B)

RELEASE END

Fig. 90 Release Hitch (Top Load)

adjustable knot (fig. 91)

The practical experience of Bob Chisnall is evident, once again, in this excellent slide-and-lock knot. The Adjustable Loop (fig. 91(A)) will slide easily in either direction, but locks up firmly under load; after release of the load it may once again be slid along the rope. Two of the knots will make an Adjustable Bend (fig. 91(B)); and, in a single piece of line, this would create an Adjustable Strop or Sling (fig. 91(C)).

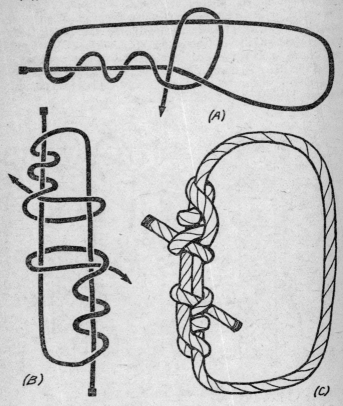

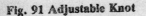

Fig. 91 Adjustable Knot

vibration proof hitch (fig. 92)
This interesting idea came from Amory Bloch Lovins, and he is the man who spotted that Hunter's Bend (fig. 85) was

actually Phil Smith's Rigger's Bend. Mr. Lovins, after 12 years guiding in the White Mountains of New Hampshire and teaching woodcraft in Maine, had certainly picked up some knots and tying methods new to me. His Vibration Proof Hitch lays up well (fig. 92(A)–(C)) only if the spar around which it is formed is fairly large relative to the diameter of the line. Then vibration by anything attached to the standing part (e.g. a flapping sail) will only tighten it owing to a double ratchet action within the knot parts.

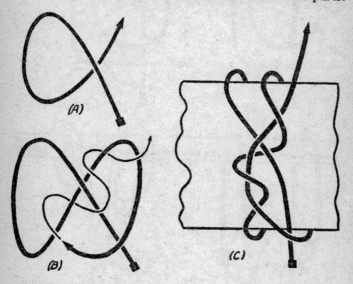

Fig. 92 Vibration proof Hitch

Julie's hitch (fig. 93)

In 1974, my younger daughter Julie – who was then 9 years old – invented this knot (fig. 93(A)–(C)) herself. It is stable, easily learnt, and seems original. With a couple of adjustments both loops can be enlarged or made smaller; or one of the two splayed bights may be enlarged at the expense of the other. There is an excellent practical use for it . . . attaching tow ropes to broken down vehicles (see car tow ropes, page 122). NOTE – the working end must be attached to the standing part with a Bowline (fig. 93(D)).

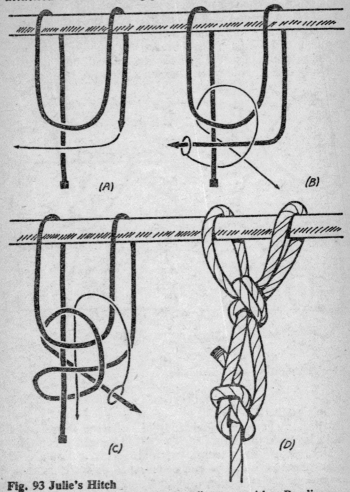

(A) *(B)* *(C)* *(D)*

Fig. 93 Julie's Hitch
Secure the working end to the standing part with a Bowline.

three quarter figure of eight loops (fig. 94)

These two variations (fig. 94(A)–(B)) of the Figure of Eight Loop (fig. 70) so popular with climbers these days, have the advantage that the ends can be pulled in opposite directions – a situation which is often necessary – without distorting the knots.

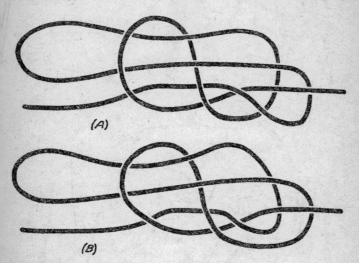

(A)

(B)

Fig. 94 Three Quarter Figure of Eight Loops

11
TRICKS

The best string tricks work like magic every time, without any special skill or preparation. Many of those I've chosen cannot fail to puzzle onlookers of any age, but the real test

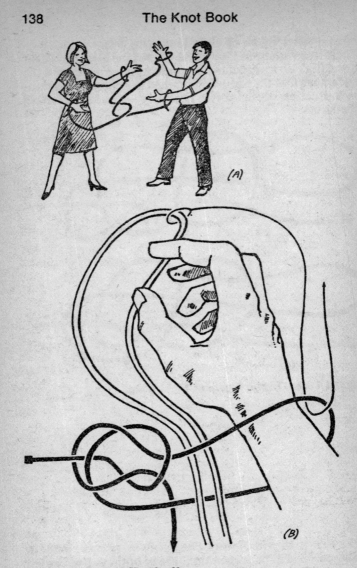

Fig. 95 Interlocked Handcuffs

is whether parents can amuse small children at parties. I believe the following will work for you . . . they do for me.

INTERLOCKING HANDCUFFS (fig. 95)

Party organisers should take note of this. Bowlines (fig. 13) are used for make-belief handcuffs. They needn't be tight. Two volunteers are linked together (fig. 95(A)) and challenged to separate without either cutting the line, untying the knots, or slipping the loops off their wrists.

Young children love it; and, with very little encouragement, will climb in and out of the large bights and turn somersaults through each other's arms in ingenious efforts to free themselves (the length of each line should be about 1½ metres to permit these antics). Onlookers will find it fun. It can be an ice-breaker at adult parties too.

The solution — passing a bight under one wrist loop (fig. 95(B)) and then over the hand of the captive — is even funnier for being so unspectacular.

OVERHAND KNOTS GALORE (fig. 96)

I like this one because it's the nearest to magician's sleight of hand I can achieve . . . but it's really very easy. Build up a series of half-hitches on your thumb (fig. 96(A)) until it's full (the thinner the cord, the more half-hitches, and the better the impression). Trap the working end atop your thumb with a nearby finger, and carefully draw all those half-hitches off your thumb (fig. 96(B)); at the same time carry that trapped end through the tunnel formed by the half-hitches until it comes out at the other end.

Transfer the bunched-up bird's nest of half-formed knots gently in the palm of your hand, surrounding it with your fingers so that only the arrowed end sticks up out of your grasp. Take that end between the fingers of your free hand and steadily draw it out. Overhand knots will appear (fig. 96(C)), neatly spaced, one after the other. If at any time you sense a slight snag within the remaining concealed half-hitches, which could develop into a hopeless tangle, manipulation with your fingers will resolve it. You must tell some far-fetched yarn as you tie the knots . . . such as how you became the Knotting Champion of the World. (This trick has a very practical application. Merchant Navy seamen used to improvise climbing ropes by throwing them over the ship's side in coils so that the knots appeared as they fell; and Fire Brigades in Britain and the U.S.A. have been shown the method.)

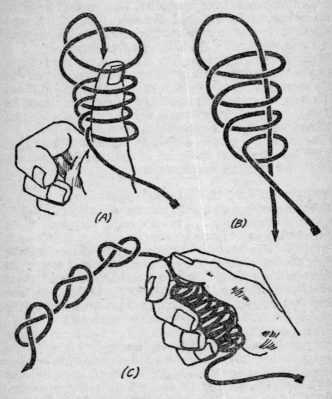

(A)

(B)

(C)

Fig. 96 Overhand Knots Galore

RELEASING THE SCISSORS (fig. 97)
Many knotted string release tricks are based upon the principle of drawing slack out of a hitch, and passing the

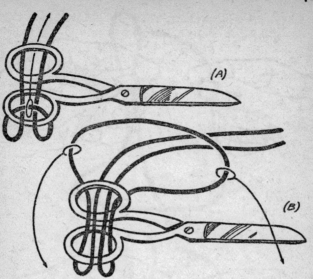

Fig. 97 Releasing the Scissors

bight obtained over the object to be freed. It works with rings, and keys, and the button holes in garments. Scissors have the seemingly added complication of the line passing through the fingerholds. It makes no difference. The challenge is always to free the item held without touching the free ends of the string.

THREADING THE NEEDLE (fig. 98)
This clever little illusion cannot fail to outwit. Show a small bight of cord between finger and thumb, with your other hand pointing the free end of the cord at the bight and attempting to poke it through (fig. 98(A)) . . . like threading a needle. Explain that you will get it through without letting go of the end, although the bight is clearly seen to be too small to permit the passage of your fist.

Then add that, "to make it even harder", you will alter the set-up slightly. Take a great many turns around the

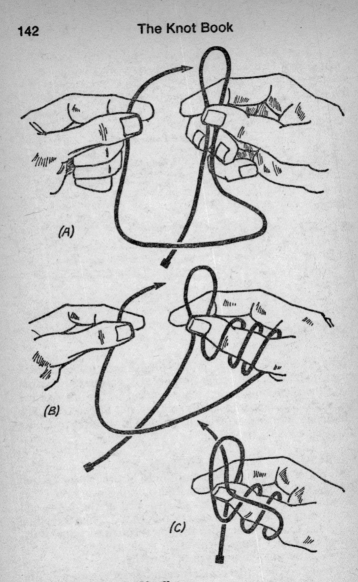

(A)

(B)

(C)

Fig. 98 Threading the Needle

thumb before forming the bight (fig. 98(B)). Pick up the end again and — after a few preliminary practice passes, — suddenly dart the hand forward (taking care to pass it to the side of the bight by the end of the thumb). Loosen momentarily the grip you have on the bight, letting the cord slip around the end of your thumb and into the bight from below. The back of your hand and fingers mask this, and — anyway — it occurs too fast for an unprepared eye to follow. Your audience will see the end threaded through the bight, still in your hand; but fail to notice that the bight has reversed itself and that one of the turns around your thumb has vanished (fig. 98(C)).

UNFOLDING A KNOT (fig. 99)

Not for an adult audience, this will intrigue small children. A length of string, or a table napkin, is laid out. The trick is to hold one end in each hand and then to tie a knot without letting go of those ends. The solution is to fold your arms (fig. 99(A)) (which ties them in a knot) before picking up the ends. Then, as the arms unfold, the overhand knot which they formed is transferred to the string or napkin (fig. 99(B)).

Fig. 99 Unfolding a Knot

A DISAPPEARING KNOT (fig. 100)

Loosely, and with great deliberation, demonstrate tying the two halves of a Reef Knot (fig. 100(A)). Then further interweave and tuck (fig. 100(B)) one of the working ends "to make it really secure". Keep the creation loose. Although it looks complicated, a steady pull on the ends will cause it to fall apart leaving the cord unknotted once again.

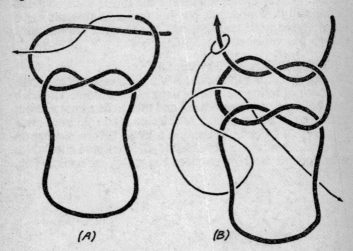

(A)   (B)

Fig. 100 A Disappearing Knot

THE WORLD'S WORST KNOT (fig. 101)

This bend (fig. 101(A)–(B)) is a combination of the Thief Knot and the Granny Knot with the weakness of both, so it slips and slides with little chance of it jamming at all. Perhaps it should be called a 'Greef' Knot, for whoever trusted in it would soon come to grief! Tied in two smooth and flexible cords it can be made to travel steadily down both lines by pulling them apart (fig. 101(C)–(E)). The demonstration is particularly effective if different coloured cords are used. Watch the two parts of the line which come

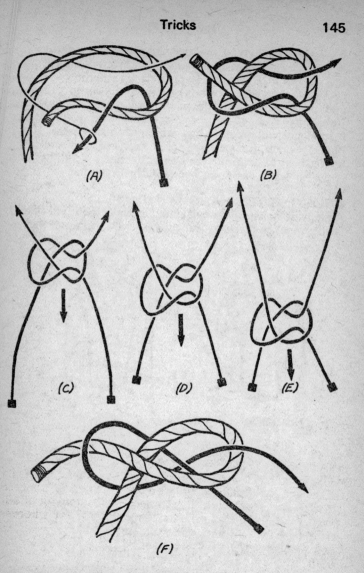

Fig. 101 The World's Worst Knot

from the underside of the knot. If they change places (fig. 101(F)), then the knot will jam . . . and your demonstration will be spoilt. Prevent it happening by standing with one foot casually placed on a box or step, with your thigh raised, and one line hanging down on either side of your leg. Imparting a slight twist to each end with your fingers (experience will quickly show which way) also helps. If the knot does jam, just pass the cords to one of your audience, invite them to continue the demonstration . . . and blame them for what has gone wrong with the knot.

CHEATING THE HANGMAN (fig. 102)

A grisly demonstration, calculated to make the timid flinch. Discourage children from copying you because this is

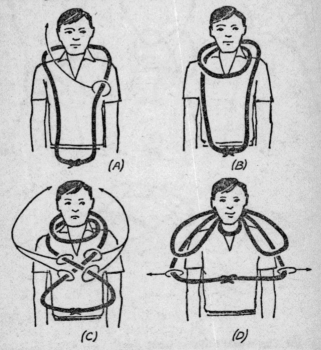

Fig. 102 Cheating the Hangman

obviously a trick which could be fatal to anyone who didn't know exactly how to do it. Keep a razor-sharp knife close to hand and always have another person who knows where it is and when to use it (see page 34) . . . just in case. (Having delivered that caution, let me reassure you I've done the trick innumerable times without incident and I've never known anyone in trouble as a result of my example).

Knot about 2 metres of line using a Reef Knot (fig. 12) and suspend the endless loop around your neck (fig. 102(A)). Take a round turn (and keep the knot as far away from your neck as possible) (fig. 102(B)). Pause, and pull tentatively with both hands to show that at this stage strangulation is a real possibility. Cross the two lower parts of the loop on your chest (do it precisely as shown) (fig. 102(C)) and lift the lower loop so formed clean over your head. Pull the two parts of the loop sharply sideways (fig. 102(D)), and − far from throttling you − the line will instantly separate from your neck, leaving you unharmed.

FIND THE MIDDLE (fig. 103)
This gimmick has been operated for centuries by fair ground swindlers to separate the simple from their money. It works best with a man's leather belt.

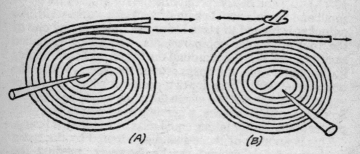

(A)   *(B)*

Fig. 103 Find the Middle

Double the belt in half, forming a tight loop in the middle, then roll it up snugly and hold it on a flat surface. Note that two identical tear-shaped spaces have been created at the centre of the roll. One is, of course, the loop in the middle

of the belt but the closer you study them the harder it is to
be certain which of the two it really is (n.b. take care not
to use a belt with distinctive light and dark sides, or
patterned and plain, for this would be a sure guide to a
quick, calculating mind).

Invite the punter to insert a pencil or other pointer into
the loop formed at the middle of the belt. If he chooses
correctly, then when you pull away the ends of the belt his
pencil should trap the belt by the loop. If wrong, the belt
will slip around it and remain free.

But . . . here's how you, the operator, can win every time.
Firstly, *you* must be certain just which is the real loop!
Secondly, you vary the routine imperceptibly depending
upon which selection your punter makes. Should they choose
the wrong space (fig. 103(B)), no problem; just pull both
ends away together. But if they do select the right loop (fig.
103(A)), then defeat them by taking the outer end and
pulling the two ends away in opposite directions. Once more
they will fail and lose. The way to pull in this case is shown
by fig. 103(B).

THE FINGER TRAP (fig. 104)

A knotted cord is tossed casually down onto the table (fig.
104(A)–(B)) and deftly spread into the rectangular form. (A
small and flexible metal chain or necklace works well). An
onlooker is invited to place his or her finger in any one of
the four triangular compartments. The string is pulled
smartly away. If it slides around the finger, without trapping
it, the punter wins. If it snags around the finger, you — the
operator — win. There are two positions where the finger
would be caught and two where the string would be released.
So this is a 50/50 chance, a genuine even-money bet, with
punter and operator taking equal risks of winning or losing.

This is another of those swindles adopted by the street
market and fair ground sharks, however, because the
percentage can be switched in their favour. With an
unnoticed twist of the wrist, just before the downward
pointing loop is laid over the sideways one, the cord can
be thrown down in a different layout (fig. 104(C)–(D)) which
is quickly spread to look just like the first game. Notice,

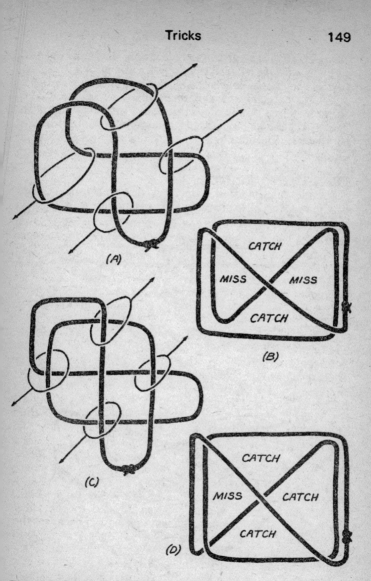

Fig. 104 The Finger Trap

however, that there are now three places where the operator can win, compared with only one for the poor old punter. Just as they begin to get the hang of it, at least one of the compartments changes its nature to catch or release. Played for money in a public place this could get you arrested for unlawful gaming but played privately amongst friends — for pennies or matches — it can cause some hilarious moments.

FREE THE RING (fig. 105)

A simple manipulation, this can be done quicker than thought after a little practice. Pass the endless loop through

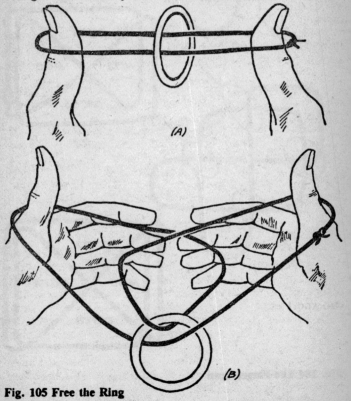

Fig. 105 Free the Ring

the ring (fig. 105(A)). It works just as well with scissors, a key, or someone's buttonhole. Suspend the loop on both thumbs as shown, and then pick up a bight with each little finger in turn, exactly as shown (fig. 105(B)). Cast off the loop from the left hand's little finger and the right hand's thumb at the same moment . . . and pull the hands smartly apart. Faster than onlookers can see or understand, the ring will drop from the cord as though cut through by it.

CUTTING AND RESTORING ROPE (fig. 106)

A piece of cord is doubled, the loop thus formed is cut with scissors or a knife . . . and seconds later the audience can examine the same piece of line, now apparently rejoined invisibly.

This is a classic illusion and professional magicians have evolved over 100 skilled methods of presenting the trick. Just as you think you've figured out how it's done, they switch to another method. Some need gimmicky ropes with concealed fastenings. Others depend upon the skill to palm spare sliding knots. Occasionally it can only be done upon a stage.

I can survive happily with young audiences on just 2 of the straightforward versions which need no special skill or preparation; these follow. Display an intact piece of magician's cord (white cotton braided rope or the manmade fibre equivalent) about 2 metres long. Double it, explaining the need to find the exact centre of the line, and hold the two ends close together, pointing upwards, between thumb and fingers . . . with the back of your hand towards your audience (you are going to do something behind that hand that you don't want seen). Locate the middle of the cord as it dangles down in front of you and pick up the bight over your free thumb and finger (fig. 106(A)). Ostensibly, place the bight forming the middle of the cord beside the two short ends poking up already in full view. In fact, surreptitiously (and in a smooth uninterrupted pass of your hand) pick up a part of the cord below one of the short ends . . . and form this into a visible bight (fig. 106(B)) which falsely represents the middle of the rope. What you have just done should be completely masked by your innocent hand holding up the ends.

Cut the line, claiming you are cutting it in half, although really you are only snipping off a few centimetres at one end. The rest is showmanship. You may lick the cut ends (magic glue!) prior to tucking them down into your fist to be sealed back together; or sprinkle invisible sticky dust over them and mutter incantations. Suddenly, toss the intact line out into your audience for inspection. Focusing on the flying line will take their eyes away from you as you pocket that

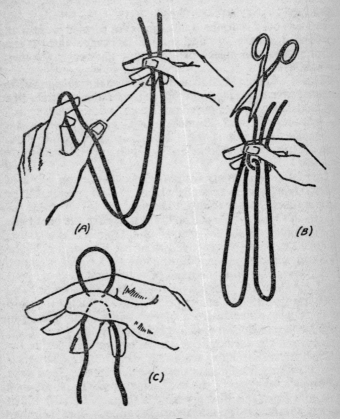

(A)

(B)

(C)

Fig. 106 Cutting and Restoring Rope

short off-cut of cord, or deposit it in a nearby vase.

Once is never sufficient for this trick. You must repeat it. Having shown clearly on the first occasion that you had nothing concealed in your hands, you could safely retain that off-cut from the first cut to use in version number two. This time, to quell the suspicion of those who wonder why you held the cord in such a contrived way before, simply pick up the cord by its approximate middle (with the ends now dangling downwards) and place it directly in your other hand with the bight representing the centre on view. Only, once again, it's a false bight (fig. 106(C)). You've bent the off-cut over into an upside-down 'U'-shape and it's that which the audience can see.

Cut it, throw out the rope for inspection, and dispose of the two smaller off-cuts. (Since the line loses a few centimetres each time you cut, you will need 2 metres or so if the missing portions are to go unnoticed).

GLOSSARY

ABSEIL — the act of riding down an anchored climbing rope in a self-controlled descent (also called 'rappelling').
ANCHOR — quite apart from its usual meaning, the term 'anchor' used in regard to knotting rope (particularly climbers' ropes) means 'belaying' (see below) for safety purposes.

BARREL KNOT — see 'Blood Knot'.
BELAY — winding a rope under load in a figure-of-eight pattern around a fixture to make the rope fast. Climbers use the term somewhat differently; for them belaying is protecting or controlling themselves with a safety line.
BEND — a knot which ties two free ropes' ends together, or the action of knotting two ropes together (same origin as the word 'bind').
BIGHT — the slack part of a rope between either end and the standing part, particularly when it forms a loop or partial loop. Knots tied "in the bight" or "on the bight" do not need the ends for the tying process.
BLOOD KNOT (or Barrel Knot) — any one of a group of knots, used especially by anglers, with numerous wrapping turns (giving them a barrel-shaped appearance) to keep a relatively high breaking strength.
BREAKING STRENGTH (B.S.) — an estimation of the load which it has been calculated by manufacturers will cause a rope to part. It takes no account of wear and tear, shock loading, or weakening by knots, and is not the safe working load (see also that heading).

CABLE — any large rope or anchor warp (or chain) is called a cable; but 'cable-laid' rope is three righthanded hawsers laid up lefthanded to form a larger 9-stranded rope or cable.
CAPSIZE — to distort a knot by tugging or overloading it so that it loses its characteristic layout. It may be a fault causing the knot to weaken or spill apart, but can be done deliberately to some knots as a quick way of tying or untying them.

CORD – strictly, this is several tightly twisted yarns making small line under 10mm. diameter; but 'cordage' is a comprehensive word for all line of whatever size or material which has no special purpose.

CORE – the loosely twisted strand, or bundle of parallel yarns or filaments, running the length of larger ropes to form an inner heart or filler. Found in ropes of more than 3 strands and in most braided lines, it may simply be a cheap filler of weak stuff; or it could have a specific role as a stiffener or reinforcer.

DOG – to wind the tail end of a rope back several times around itself or another rope (often larger), with the lay, to secure it temporarily against a lengthwise pull. A draw-loop prevented from undoing accidentally, either by whipping it or by poking something through it, is also often said to be 'dogged'.

EIGHT PLAIT – rope of the larger sizes made up of 4 pairs of strands, two spiralling clockwise and two anticlockwise; it is strong but flexible and will not kink.

END – usually the end of line which is being knotted, whipped, etc., more precisely called the 'running end' or 'working end' or 'free end' (see also 'Standing End').

EYE – a loop usually made in the end of rope by splicing it.

FIBRE – the natural vegetable equivalent of filaments; the smallest element of rope construction, twisted to make yarns.

FILAMENT – the smallest element of material forming the individual fibres of synthetic rope.

HARD LAID – rope made tightly twisted.

HAWSER – strictly, any very large rope over about 40mm. diameter, which is not a cable, big enough for towing or mooring; but generally refers to all three strand righthanded ropes.

HEART – see 'Core'.

HITCH – a knot that secures a rope to a post, ring, spar or rail, etc., or to another rope which takes no part in tying the knot. It won't keep shape on its own. In climbers' jargon, a 'hitch' is often just a temporary fastening.

KARABINER (carabiner, krab. or crab.) — a metal snaplink used by climbers as an attachment for ropes.

KERNMANTEL ROPE — sheath and core climbers' rope designed to absorb shock elastically.

KNOT — the word is used to cover every kind of occasion where the end of a line is passed through a loop in itself. But 'Knots' are also a special group of knots separate from 'bends' and 'hitches', in which case knots are only (a) binding knots, (b) stopper knots in the end of line, (c) knots forming loops or nooses, and (d) knots joining small lines together (which are usually referred to as bends), or both ends of the same small line.

LANYARD — a small line, often braided and ornamental, attached to knives and other personal items of equipment to prevent their loss. Also a line used to secure and tighten rigging on sailing vessels.

LAY — the direction, either lefthanded or righthanded, of twist in the strands of rope; also the nature (tight, medium, or loose) of that twist.

LEAD (pronounced 'leed') — the direction taken by the working end through any knot, giving an indication of how it was tied, or of a rope around an object.

LINE — a general label for most cordage with no special purpose. Alternatively, it is used to refer to rope with a purpose, e.g. clothes line, heaving line, fishing line.

LOOP — a part of the rope bent so that its parts come together or actually cross.

MAKE FAST — to secure a rope with a hitch, or to belay (see also that heading).

MESSENGER — a light line passed or thrown in advance of a heavier rope, etc., which it will then haul or hoist across an intervening gap.

MIDDLE — to fold a line into two equal parts to locate the centre.

NATURAL ROPE – cordage of all kinds made from vegetable fibres.

NIP – the binding, frictional pressure within a knot preventing it slipping; a sharp turn in a rope creating the point in a knot where parts grip each other.

NOOSE – a loop secured around its own standing part as a slip knot which pulls tight.

PARBUCKLE – an arrangement of the ends of a single rope around a cylindrical object so as to lift or lower it by a rolling movement.

RAPPEL – see 'Abseil'.

REEF – shortening sail, i.e. reducing its surface area to cope with strengthening winds; traditionally achieved by bunching the sail and parcelling it up at intervals with short lengths of line sewn onto the sail at regular points . . . using reef knots.

REEVE – to pass the end of a rope through any aperture, like when making up a block and tackle.

ROPE – any cordage over 10mm. diameter.

'S' LAID ROPE – lefthanded rope.

SAFE WORKING LOAD (S.W.L.) – the estimated load which can be placed upon a rope without it breaking, taking account of its age, condition, the knots used, and the possibility of shock loading. S.W.L. may be as little as one sixth the quoted breaking strength (see also that heading).

SECURITY – a knot's inherent ability to resist slipping, distorting or capsizing under load or intermittent jerking . . . a quality quite distinct from 'Strength' (see also that heading).

SLING – rope, wire or webbing put around an object, usually in the form of an endless band (best spliced but sometimes knotted), to hoist or haul it; often called a 'Strop' (see also that heading). Climbers may call an extra loop attachment for their climbing ropes a sling.

SMALL STUFF – line under 10mm. diameter, but especially cord, string, thread and the like.

SOFT LAID – loosely twisted rope.

STANDING END — the opposite end to the working end (see also 'End').

STANDING PART — the part of a rope not being handled or worked, as opposed to the ends or a bight.

STAPLE — graded fibres or chopped filaments for ropemaking (rope made from staple has a fibrous or fuzzy surface due to all the ends).

STRAND — yarns twisted together in the opposite direction to that of the yarn itself; a major element in the complete rope. Rope made with strands — not braided — is 'laid line'. 'Stranded' rope has one strand broken or severely damaged.

STRENGTH — the knot's capacity to withstand a load without breaking the line . . . distinctly different to 'Security' (see also that heading).

STRING — thick thread, twine, thin cordage, usually for domestic use.

STROP — strictly, the rope or wire band (or strap) seized around a pulley block to suspend it; the word is often used for a 'Sling' (see also that heading).

SYNTHETIC ROPE — rope made from manmade filaments or staples.

TAKING A TURN — leading a rope around a bollard or other fixing for friction prior to belaying.

THREAD — a yarn; otherwise, fine line for sewing.

WARP — to move a vessel by means of hawsers; so, warps may be hawsers for that purpose or mooring lines. Weavers' warps are the threads running lengthwise in weaving.

WEFT — the transverse weaving threads.

WHIPPING — to wrap the end of rope tightly with small stuff to prevent it unlaying and fraying.

WORKING END — see 'End'.

YARN — any number of individual fibres or filaments twisted together as the first stage in ropemaking.

'Z' LAID ROPE — righthanded rope.

THE INTERNATIONAL GUILD OF KNOT TYERS

The Guild grew from an idea by Des Pawson, an Ipswich knot craftsman, and the author. At the inaugural meeting aboard the Maritime Trust's vessel R.R.S. 'Discovery' berthed near Tower Bridge, in April, 1982, twenty-five founder members voted unanimously to go ahead with the scheme. A steering committee was appointed and constitutional rules, membership conditions, etc., agreed.

The Guild's objects are ". . . to promote the art, craft and science of knotting, its study and practice; to undertake research into all aspects of knotting; and to establish an authoritative body for consultative purposes."

Membership is open to anyone interested in knotting (whether expert or simply hoping to learn from others) and has grown fast to include established authors and consultants of knotting, a lady sail-maker and another who ties bellropes, Sea Scouts and Rangers, a titled gentleman and a number of the Magic Circle, as well as numerous boat owners, with representatives in the U.S.A., Australia, Europe and Asia.

The members keep in touch through a quarterly newsletter and a couple of meetings a year, but regional groups may meet more often. The annual subscription is modest, aiming simply to cover costs.

If you'd like to know more, contact the Guild through the author of this book, Geoffrey BUDWORTH, 7, Hazel Shaw, TONBRIDGE, Kent, TN10 3QE, U.K.

OUR PUBLISHING POLICY

HOW WE CHOOSE

Our policy is to consider every deserving manuscript and we can give special editorial help where an author is an authority on his subject but an inexperienced writer. We are rigorously selective in the choice of books we publish. We set the highest standards of editorial quality and accuracy. This means that a *Paperfront* is easy to understand and delightful to read. Where illustrations are necessary to convey points of detail, these are drawn up by a subject specialist artist from our panel.

HOW WE KEEP PRICES LOW

We aim for the big seller. This enables us to order enormous print runs and achieve the lowest price for you. Unfortunately, this means that you will not find in the *Paperfront* list any titles on obscure subjects of minority interest only. These could not be printed in large enough quantities to be sold for the low price at which we offer this series.

We sell almost all our *Paperfronts* at the same unit price. This saves a lot of fiddling about in our clerical departments and helps us to give you world-beating value. Under this system, the longer titles are offered at a price which we believe to be unmatched by any publisher in the world.

OUR DISTRIBUTION SYSTEM

Because of the competitive price, and the rapid turnover, *Paperfronts* are possibly the most profitable line a bookseller can handle. They are stocked by the best bookshops all over the world. It may be that your bookseller has run out of stock of a particular title. If so, he can order more from us at any time—we have a fine reputation for "same day" despatch, and we supply any order, however small (even a single copy), to any bookseller who has an account with us. We prefer you to buy from your bookseller, as this reminds him of the strong underlying public demand for *Paperfronts*. Members of the public who live in remote places, or who are housebound, or whose local bookseller is unco-operative, can order direct from us by post.

FREE

If you would like an up-to-date list of all paperfront titles currently available, send a stamped self-addressed envelope to
ELLIOT RIGHT WAY BOOKS, BRIGHTON RD.,
LOWER KINGSWOOD, SURREY, U.K.